BMC 1100/1300 (ADO16

Austin, Morris, MG, Riley, Wolseley and Vanden Pl...

Also from Veloce:

A Pictorial History (series)
Austin Cars 1948 to 1990 (Rowe)
Citroën Cars 1934 to 1986 (Parish)
Ford Cars – Ford UK cars 1945-1995 (Rowe)
Jaguar Cars 1946 to 2008 (Thorley)
Mercedes-Benz Cars 1947 to 2000 (Taylor)
Morris Cars 1948 to 1984 (Newell)
Riley & Wolseley Cars 1948 to 1975 (Rowe)
Rootes Cars of the 50s, 60s & 70s – Hillman, Humber, Singer, Sunbeam & Talbot (Rowe)
Rover Cars 1945 to 2005 (Taylor)
Triumph & Standard Cars 1945 to 1984 (Warrington)
Vauxhall Cars 1945 to 1995 (Alder)
Volvo Cars 1945 to 1985 (Alder)

www.veloce.co.uk

First published in June 2024 by Veloce, an imprint of David and Charles Limited. Tel +44 (0)1305 260068 / email info@veloce.co.uk / web www.veloce.co.uk.

BMC 1100/1300 (ADO16)

Austin, Morris, MG, Riley, Wolseley and Vanden Plas

Matthew Vale

Contents

Foreword & Acknowledgements

Foreword

The years when the ADO16 range was sold new was an age when The Beatles dominated the charts, James Bond was on every cinema screen, US and USSR rockets jostled for dominance in space, and the Cold War simmered away in the background. The ADO16 was pretty much ubiquitous in Britain. No matter where you went there would be one lurking by the kerb, driving down the road, or sitting on a suburban drive.

Watch any UK-based TV series from the time and the hero would be driving a fast and elegant British coupé and the baddies would be driving some lumpen continental saloon. There would, however, be a Morris or Austin 1100 in virtually every street scene. This is hardly surprising, given that the car was the UK's best-seller every year from 1963 to 1971 (except for 1967 when Ford's Cortina pipped it to the post).

Even today the car still intrudes into popular culture. It had a fleeting role in the 2019 cartoon *The Tiger Who Came to Tea*, based on the book by Judith Kerr. A mustard yellow four-door is seen driving past the café where the family are having their sausages and chip supper after the tiger had eaten all the food in the house.

The reason for this popularity was that the ADO16 range was, arguably, the de-facto British family car, with small dimensions and engines, but enough space and performance to carry out the task of safe, reliable and economical transport for the nuclear family of the time. The designers achieved this by exploiting, but not shouting about, some very advanced thinking. The car combined clever engineering technology, in the shape of sophisticated Hydrolastic suspension, very compact engines and gearboxes, great body design, which gave amazing space for the passengers within the relatively small dimensions, and good looks, thanks to Italian coachbuilder Carrozzeria Pininfarina's up-to-the-minute styling.

While the range may not have had the sporting pretensions of some rivals, or the mechanical simplicity of others, the cars got on with the job, providing day-to-day service to millions of drivers across the world, with minimal drama and cost.

In the classic car scene of today ADO16 still does not have the popularity or cachet of the traditional MG and Triumph sports cars, with their wind in the hair open-topped style, nor the fast Ford saloons with their race and rally pedigree, or even the cheeky 'swinging sixties' vibe of the original Mini.

It is a fact that, in the early days of the classic car scene, those practical family cars of the '60s and early '70s were

The Mark I ADO16 is exemplified here with this shot of Jim Hills' MG. With a peppy twin-carburettor engine, two-tone paintwork, and distinctive MG chrome radiator grille, the MG version of ADO16 sold well in both home and export markets.

not a popular choice as a classic car. In the 1980s and 1990s an ADO16 was seen as a disposable banger. If (not when) an example needed work – especially costly bodywork – it was just not worth spending any real money on it, as its street value was low and there were plenty of other cheap examples available.

Indeed, in the mid 1980s when the author sold his classic sports cars, an MGB and Triumph Spitfire Mark III, to raise the deposit on his first house, he then ran a 1967 Austin 1100 that he bought for a couple of hundred quid. The car did sterling service for a year or so, it was cheap to buy and run, but when

the rear subframe mounts rotted out (giving rise to the rear tyres wearing out quicker than the front) it made no financial sense to repair it and so was scrapped. Its replacement was an equally dog-eared, but younger and less rusty, Morris Marina 1300cc two-door coupé from the same BMC/British Leyland stable, which again gave good service and was sold on when finances improved.

Many ADO16s met the same fate and were scrapped, but the good news is that, as so many were produced, a fair few have survived, and today they are still around in reasonable numbers

Dean Oakey's 1971 Morris 1300 Mark II shows off its Limeflower paintwork. By the 1970s, ADO16 was looking a bit dated, so British Leyland jazzed up the cars with new paint colours.

and often in excellent condition. ADO16's undoubted qualities are *finally* beginning to be recognised.

This book, then, is a celebration of the ADO16. In their day the cars were best-sellers, gave lots of British families their first truly modern, stylish and practical car, and were a reliable, economical and roomy all-rounder. With over a million sold in the UK between 1962 and 1973, they were pretty much the 'Universal British Car' of the time, and were present in every city, town, and village, and on every country road and trunk route in the '60s. And who can forget Basil Fawlty giving his

estate version a 'damn good thrashing' with a tree branch in an episode of *Fawlty Towers*?

Let's celebrate one of the British motor industry's forgotten successes, the car that built on the success of the Mini to provide Britain and the rest of the world with a little gem of a motor (but not so little inside), and the perfect family saloon car of the time.

Acknowledgements

Thanks are due to the following members of the 1100 Club:

David Haycock, Dean Oakey, John Norris and Roy Robinson, all of whom kindly allowed the author to interview them about their ADO16 stories, and to photograph their cars for the book. Thanks also to my good friend Jim Hills, whose immaculate and original MG 1100 also features, and Dave Groves, who kindly supplied the pictures of the Magenta kit car he built.

The production number data used in this book is based on the work of Chris Morris, 1100 Club Historian, and reproduced from the 1100 Club's book *The Story of the BMC 1100*, compiled, designed and typeset by Fernand U A Pinckney, the 1100 Club Regalia Secretary.

www.veloce.co.uk / www.velocebooks.com
All current books • New book news • Special offers • Gift vouchers

Chapter 1

Introduction to the ADO16 range

Introduction

The Austin/Morris 1100/1300 range was the British Motor Corporation's (BMC) small family saloon car for the 1960s, sitting above the Mini and, initially, below the Austin Cambridge and Morris Oxford 'Farina' saloons, and then later the Austin Morris 1800 'Landcrab' range. As such, the range was a vital product for BMC, and such was its success that it was Britain's best selling car virtually every year after its introduction through to the 1970s.

Introduced in 1962, the

This is a factory publicity shot of the Mark II Austin 1100 from the mid-1960s. The car's crisp lines and unfussy styling are obvious; less so is the slightly truncated rear wings that were the main change to the bodywork for the Mark II.

range was designated ADO16 by the factory – ADO standing for Austin Drawing Office, and 16 being the project number. Some sources suggest that ADO stands for 'Amalgamated Design Office': it's unclear which is correct.

During the late 1950s and 1960s, BMC's design projects included: ADO15 (the Mini, introduced in 1959); ADO16

David Haycock's 1966 Mark I Riley Kestrel shows off its two-tone paintwork.

(the 1100/1300 range introduced in 1962); ADO17 (introduced in 1964 was the bigger, four-door Austin/Morris 1800 nicknamed the 'Landcrab'); and ADO14 (the Maxi, introduced in 1969 and originally conceived as a car sized to fit between the ADO16 and ADO17, eventually emerging as a five-door hatchback sold alongside the 'Landcrab' and ADO16 in 1969).

As can be seen from these cars and dates, the project that took the longest to come to fruition was the Maxi (ADO14), which suffered from numerous rethinks and redesigns before being rushed into production when British Leyland was created with the merger of British Motor Holdings (BMC plus Jaguar and body manufacturer Pressed Steel) and Leyland Motors (Standard Triumph, Rover, Alvis and Leyland Commercial Vehicles) in 1968.

However, all this was in the future, as 1962 saw the introduction of ADO16 in Morris and MG forms. ADO16 was a logical extension of the Mini, using the layout and many of the mechanical elements of that brilliant small car, but redesigned as a medium-sized family car: large enough to easily carry a family of four and luggage; small and light enough to be nimble and economical to run; and, probably most importantly, reasonably cheap to buy.

In the first road test of ADO16, in Morris 1100 guise, *Autocar* (17th August 1962 issue) stated:

"On its behaviour, conclusive opinions have been formed; the unanimous view of the test staff is that on an overall rating for ride comfort on smooth or rough roads at all speeds, controllability in these conditions, adhesion in the wet or dry, inherent safety and steering response, there is no better car, irrespective of size."

This is high praise indeed, and underlines a major truth about the whole ADO16 family of cars: the suspension system, combined with the stiff and strong monocoque body, gave the best possible combination of ride, handling and comfort that the road testers had come across.

The fact that this was in a compact five-seat family car with a price that put it in reach of the average family man, rather than some exotic sports or GT car was all the more astounding. It shows how advanced ADO16 was, both as a concept and in the flesh, and really was a tribute to the design team who managed to produce such an outstanding car.

British Motor Corporation

In order to understand the ADO16, it is important to understand the background of the company under which the car was designed, and then the evolution of the company into what would eventually become the behemoth that was British Leyland.

In 1952, two of the biggest mainstream car manufacturers – The Austin Motor Company Ltd and Morris Motors Ltd – merged to form the largest British car manufacturer of the time. The new organisation was headquartered at the newly modified Austin plant at Longbridge in Birmingham, and, while the first chairman of the organisation was Lord Nuffield (William Morris), the head of Morris before the amalgamation, he was soon replaced by Austin's chairman Leonard Lord.

The consolidation and integration of the two large organisations occurred with aching slowness, and, while most Morris-based engines were dropped fairly quickly in favour of Austin's A- and B-series units, many of the old model names inherited from Morris' record of acquisitions remained in use, and the practice of 'badge engineering' became commonplace. The new organisation's large number of manufacturing sites also meant that competing ranges of cars (for example, the Austin A40 and Morris Minor) continued to be produced and sold, which made it difficult for the new organisation to capitalise on the economies of scale that the amalgamation should have generated. Even the introduction of all-new models, such as ADO16, did not stop this practice – witness the continuing production of the A40 and the Morris 1000, both of which competed for sales against ADO16 long after the latter was established. Further rationalisation came

Roy Robinson's 1971 Mark II Morris Traveller is painted in Aqua, a typical 1970s paint choice for British Leyland. The Traveller (along with its Austin stablemate, the Countryman) was the versatile three-door estate version of ADO16.

in 1965 with BMC's acquisition the major body manufacturer, Coventry-based Pressed Steel, which, in turn, led to Jaguar being brought into the fold in 1965. BMC was renamed British Motor Holdings (BMH) in 1966, and then, in 1968, with encouragement from the Government, merged with Leyland Motors in 1968 to form the virtually unmanageable leviathan that was British Leyland.

So ADO16 was designed after the creation of BMC, and, while the Mini preceded ADO16 into production thanks to the Suez crisis and the consequential increases in fuel prices, ADO16 was the first car designed specifically to replace many existing models in the BMC range.

The BMC range in 1962

Probably the most significant car in the BMC range on the introduction of ADO16 (which was originally labeled XC/9002) was the Mini. Designated ADO15 (originally XC/9003 – note that the original design number reflects that production of the Mini was moved ahead of the 1100 due to the the need for a very fuel efficient small car) and introduced in 1959, the Mini was produced in response to the Suez crisis of the late 1950s, when fuel prices rocketed after Britain and France launched an abortive sortie to reclaim the Suez Canal after Egypt's General Nasser privatised it.

The Issigonis-designed Mini was an innovative little car,

Bonhams

ADO16's stablemate was the Mini, which was rushed into production before ADO16 in response to the Suez crisis. ADO16 shared its layout and many mechanical features with the Mini. This Police version probably lost 10mph in top speed with the massive Police sign on its roof!

offering great space for passengers within its compact shell thanks to its clever combined engine and gearbox and its 'wheel at each corner' architecture, both features that were expanded upon in ADO16. Interestingly, the Mini did not replace any existing models in the BMC range, but rather slotted-in at the bottom of said range to offer an economical, small but 'real' car to compete against the bubble cars and microcars that had occupied that market space previously.

Sitting above the Mini in the Morris range in the late 1950s was the Minor 1000, another Issigonis design that had first emerged in 1948. Powered by a front-mounted 1098cc A-series engine, and with a live rear axle, the Minor in 1962 was offered

as a two- or four-door saloon, a two-door cabriolet, three-door estate or three-door commercial van. The equivalent Austin small saloon was the Farina-styled A40, a conventional front-engined, rear-wheel drive, two- or three-door hatchback, powered by a 948cc A-series engine. Sitting above ADO16 was the Farina-styled Morris Oxford Series VI and Austin A60 Cambridge range, both front-engined, rear drive, three-box layout, medium-sized, four-door saloons, which, like ADO16, were also produced in Riley, Wolseley and MG forms.

At the top of the BMC range in 1962 was the Austin A99/A110, powered by a six-cylinder, three-litre engine. Effectively a long-wheelbase version of the A60, with conventional front engine, rear drive layout and four-door saloon bodywork, the car was styled by Farina, and also came in Riley, Wolseley and Vanden Plas models.

Competition – internal

One interesting aspect of ADO16 was the internal competition. Such was the inertia and resistance to change within BMC, that, when ADO16 was introduced, the company continued to

The Morris Minor was supposed to be replaced by ADO16 but remained in production into the 1970s. This is an early 'lowlight' convertible – ADO16 was never offered as an open version.

was axed in 1969, but, somewhat bizarrely, the saloon continued in production up to the end of 1970, while production of the archaic Traveller version, with its characterful structural rear wood frame, continued in production until late 1971 – all the time taking sales from the much more modern ADO16 range.

At Austin, the same happened. Introduced a year after the Morris version, the Austin 1100/1300 competed directly against the Austin A40, another front-engined, rear-drive saloon, although only available in two- or three-door guise. The Farina-styled A40 was a newer design than the Morris 1000, and it was introduced in 1958. Originally a two-door, four-/five-seat design, it was later graced with a three-door estate version that had a horizontally split rear door, with the window hinged at its top, and the lower half hinged at its base. In two- or three-door format the A40 continued in production until 1967.

While this state of affairs seems insane to the casual observer, to be fair to BMC there was a fairly strong level of opposition to the 'new fangled' front-wheel drive cars from its more traditionally minded customers who were wary of the apparent complexity of the new offering. So sales of the rear-wheel drive Morris and Austin small saloons were not insignificant. Add to that that the tooling costs (certainly for

produce the dated cars, in the shape of the Morris 1000 and the Austin A40 Farina that ADO16 should have replaced.

The Morris competitor in the medium-sized saloon category was the Morris Minor 1000, a two- or four-door saloon, a three-door estate (or Traveller) version with split rear doors, or two-door convertible. All versions could seat up to five passengers in some comfort, albeit with less room than ADO16, and the car had a front-mounted A-series engine and rear-wheel drive.

Introduced in 1948 in Morris' first post war range of cars, and designed by Issigonis, the Morris 1000 was a very popular car, and was bang up to date on its introduction, although a front engine and live rear axle layout, and rather old fashioned styling, meant it was showing its age by the early 1960s. The convertible

The Morris Minor production hit 1,000,000 units by 1960. This is a 'Minor 1,000,000' limited edition model to celebrate the numbers. The car featured '1,000,000' badges and a special Lilac paint job. ADO16 went on to sell over 2,000,000 examples but never got an equivalent special edition model.

the Morris, less so for the Austin) had probably been covered by profits made before the introduction of ADO16, and the decision not to phase out the cars sooner made some sense.

Competition – external

So, while BMC was battling with itself for sales, the other UK manufacturers were active in the small saloon market. Triumph had released its Herald in 1959, which was available as a two-door saloon or coupé, as well as a three-door estate.

The Herald was nowhere near as sophisticated as ADO16, with its separate chassis, front engine rear drive layout and bolt-up body, but it did boast styling by Italian Giovanni Michelotti and independent suspension all round. Triumph's 1300, a small four-door saloon introduced in 1966, was as advanced as ADO16, with all round independent suspension, an innovative front-wheel drive system and a unitary four-door body with a proper boot. This upmarket small saloon was a premium product, which competed directly with the Riley and Wolseley badged ADO16.

One of the biggest competitors for ADO16 was Ford. Renowned for producing reliable, trustworthy and economical small saloons, in 1962 Ford's Anglia 105E was its small family saloon. With simple mechanicals, backward slanting rear window and modern 'American' styling, the Anglia, introduced in 1959, was powered by a new modern 997cc 'Kent' four-cylinder in-line four-cylinder engine, which was very under square (bore and stroke of 80.96 x 48.41cc), giving the unit the capability to rev high if needed. This unit was complemented by the 1198cc Kent unit introduced in 1962. Combine these attributes with a large dealer network and a loyal if conservative

Another rival to ADO16 was the Triumph Herald. While the Herald was not as advanced as ADO16 technically, its separate chassis and rear-wheel drive appealed to the traditionalist market.

customer base, then the Anglia, despite it only being available a a two-door saloon or three-door estate, was a real competitor to the mechanically more advanced ADO16, especially as the price was some 10% less. Ford's second contender for the family saloon market sector was the larger Cortina Mark I (1962-1966) and Mark II (1966-1970), which were both slightly larger than ADO16, and came with a choice of 1.2-litre and 1.5-litre Kent engines.

A more up-to-date competitor for ADO16 was the Ford Escort, introduced in 1967. While it retained the Anglia's front engine/rear-wheel drive layout, the new Escort came in two- or four-door saloon or three-door estate format, and was powered by the 1.1 or 1.3 versions of the Kent crossflow engine. Styling was a subtle version of the classic American influenced 'coke bottle' lines, and the car slotted into the Ford range below the Cortina, which, with the introduction of the Mark III in 1970, was moving up in the market and leaving the small family saloon segment to the Escort. As a newer design the Escort sold well, and its modern clean lines left ADO16

A much more advanced rival was the Triumph 1300, which was an upmarket, front-wheel-drive four-door saloon.

Another rival to ADO16 was the Ford Anglia. Here is Roy Robinson's example, parked up next to his Traveller and his Morris Half-Ton Van.

looking dated, which, by the late '60s, and thanks to no significant styling updates, it was.

The final domestic competitor for ADO16 was the Vauxhall Viva, in HA form up to 1966 when the HB took over. Like the Fords, the Viva was a conventional front engine, rear-wheel drive layout in a three-box saloon body. The HA was sold only in two-door form, but the HB, while initially offered as a two-door, added a three-door estate option in July 1967, and a four-door version in October 1968. The HA came with a 1057cc four-cylinder engine, while the HB was fitted with 1159cc, 1599cc or 1975cc engines.

The sales staff at BMC dealers were issued with small booklets that exhorted the benefits of the 1100 range and compared them to competitors.

BMC was not afraid to punch above its weight. In the 1962 *Selling the Morris 1100* booklet, as well identifying the advantages of the 1100 over the same-sized competitors, it also points out that the interior dimensions were competitive with the Vauxhall Victor Super and the Ford Consul Classic – both much bigger saloons than the diminutive ADO16!

Badge engineering and model positioning

The practice of badge engineering in the automotive industry came into existence when car firms with their own market niche were bought or merged with another company but the original firm's identity was maintained through different badging of a common platform. It reached a peak in the UK post World War Two when the motor industry, notably Morris and Rootes gobbled up smaller companies but kept the old brands alive. The practice was also common in the USA, with the big three manufacturers (Ford, Chrysler and General Motors) owning various brands in their own right, and producing cars with common underpinnings but different badges – including Mercury and Lincoln for Ford, Plymouth, Dodge and De Soto for Chrysler, and Pontiac, Chevrolet and Cadillac for GM.

In the UK the practice came to a head in the 1960s, with BMC (owning Austin, Morris, Riley, MG, Wolseley and Vanden Plas) and the Rootes Group (owning Humber, Hillman, Singer, Sunbeam, Talbot, and commercial makers Commer and Karrier) both producing numerous variants of the same car under different badges. Today the practice has evolved somewhat, with various manufacturers sharing platforms and drivetrains across brands and even between different manufacturers.

The ADO16 model range was extensive, and epitomised the practice of badge engineering promulgated by BMC in the 1960s. BMC was formed in 1952 with the amalgamation of the Austin Motor Company, run by a previous Morris Managing Director Leonard Lord, and Morris, run by W R Morris, later to become Baron Nuffield then Viscount Nuffield. Before the merger of the two companies, Morris had grown by acquisition and owned a number of additional active marques, which had their own market niche, dealerships and loyal customer base. These were MG, Riley, and Wolseley, and they were brought into the new BMC and their names continued to be used within

BMC issued its salesforce with this handy little booklet full of information on the new ADO16.

The sales information booklet included details of ADO16's competitors, which included cars that were a class above – as the booklet puts it, 'the big boys' – as well as other factors such as style, dimension, servicing, and price.

David Haycock's Mark I Riley 1100 shows the Riley execution of the two-tone paintwork that extends down to the window line and its long rear fins.

the consortium, while Vanden Plas had been bought by Austin in 1946 and also continued to be used.

While the likes of Ford concentrated on badging individual models in a range, reaching its apogee in the 1970s and '80s with the unadorned base model, followed by the 'L', 'GL', 'E', 'GLX' and 'Ghia' models, BMC continued to use the original manufacturer names (so in the case of the ADO16 range the Morris, Austin, Riley, MG, Wolseley and Vanden Plas) to differentiate the models in the range, a practice that came to be known as badge engineering. Differences between the various models involved trim levels, engine tune and minor bodywork changes to give each marque its own distinct identity.

In the case of ADO16, the normal day-to-day 'cooking' models were badged Austin or Morris, which were initially available in Standard or Luxe trim levels, and, by the mid-1960s were available in Luxe and De-luxe trim levels. These 'cooking' models were complemented by two performance variants sporting MG and Riley badges and, more obviously, new front grilles, and two luxury models badged Wolseley and Vanden Plas, which again had prominent front grilles. This enabled the range to cater for customers' loyalties to the various marques and dealerships, as well as addressing the buyers' needs for 'cooking', sports or prestige models, and, finally, establishing a distinct 'pecking order' to satisfy the desires of class conscious customers in the 1960s.

Sales figures and production dates

ADO16 was the best selling car in the UK between 1963 and 1971, with a brief blip in 1967 when the Ford Cortina took the crown. The figures here were derived from Austin Rover Group data and collated by Chris Morris, 1100 Club Historian and reproduced in the 1100 Club's book *The Story of the BMC 1100*, compiled, designed and typeset by Fernand U A Pinckney, the 1100 Club Regalia Secretary.

Year-on-year production – all models

Year	Home	Export	Total
1962	15,115	13,047	28,162
1963	92,770	63,159	155,929
1964	170,120	73,418	243,538
1965	163,171	64,882	228,053
1966	151,782	57,553	209,335
1967	135,213	41,817	177,030
1968	140,097	89,706	229,803
1969	149,789	92,654	242,443
1970	130,088	69,181	199,269
1971	111,476	70,584	182,060
1972	100,724	32,649	133,373
1973	46,364	32,644	79,008
1974	4446	18,743	23,189
1975	0	1788	1788
Grand total			**2,132,980**

This factory picture of the Vanden Plas shows the poshest ADO16's front grille, and the pair of driving lights fitted to the car as standard.

Totals by model types – up to 1969

The Austin and Morris models sales figures differentiated between Austin and Morris saloons and estates up to 1969. From 1970 the figures for Austin and Morris saloons were combined, and home market Morris saloons were discontinued in 1971. The table below shows sales of the various models up to the end of 1969.

Models	Home	Export	Total
Morris 1100 – 2- and 4-dr	35,9319	150,876	510,195
Morris 1300 – 2- and 4-dr	53,674	30,121	83,795
Austin 1100 – 2- and 4-dr	356,117	143,496	499,613
Austin 1300 – 2- and 4-dr	61,210	80,473	141,683
Morris 1100 Traveller	11,200	2470	13,670
Morris 1300 Traveller	9113	1704	10,817
Austin 1100 Countryman	12,976	3856	16,832
Austin 1300 Countryman	9404	1561	10,965
Morris 1300 GT (1969 only)	2588	635	3223
Austin 1300GT (1969 only)	2876	484	3360
MG 1100 – 2- & 4-dr	60,722	64,138	124,860
MG 1300 – 2- & 4-dr	13,160	7400	2056
Riley 1100 (1965 – 68)	11,008	1344	12,352
Riley 1300 (1967 – 69)	8572	551	9123
Wolseley 1100	15,402	1962	17,364
Wolseley 1300	9727	2078	11,805
Vanden Plas 1100	13,701	2306	16,007
Vanden Plas 1300	7288	781	8069

Totals by model types – 1970-1974

From 1970 the figures for Austin and Morris saloons were

combined, and home market Morris saloons were discontinued in 1971. The table below shows sales of the various models from 1970 up to the end of production in 1974.

Models	Home	Export	Total
Austin/Morris 1100 – 2- & 4-dr	197,620	53,389	161,009
Austin/Morris 1300 – 2- & 4-dr	172,596	129,877	302,473
Austin/Morris 1300 Estate	43,258	5334	48,592
Austin/Morris 1300GT	36,501	28,625	65,126
MG 1300 – 2- & 4-dr (up to 1973)	2427	5876	8348
Wolseley 1300	12,806	2805	15,611
Vanden Plas 1300	15,621	44	15,665

Production numbers – summary

As can be seen from the tables, production numbers of ADO16 were pretty high all the way through the 1960s, with, apart from 1967, in excess of 200,000 units being produced year-on-year from 1964 through to 1969.

Numbers started to drop off with the advent of the 1970s, and, by 1974 it was obvious that the cars were no longer selling in economical numbers, and production ended in 1975.

From a model perspective, the Austin and Morris 1100 Saloons (in both two- and four-door guise) sold the most units, with a total of 1,170,817 – virtually half of all the cars produced. Next up was the Austin and Morris 1300 saloons, with 527,751

The last of the line included the Morris 1300GT, the last sporty version of the ADO16. This is John Norris' lovely example.

units sold. The estate versions of the Austin and Morris models sold a healthy total of 100,876 and the Austin/Morris 1300GT sold only 65,126.

   The best seller of the badge engineered models was the MG, which, in 1100 and 1300 form sold a mighty 135,264. Next came Wolseley with 44,780 and Vanden Plas 39,741, while the Riley 1100 and 1300 brought up the rear with sales totalling only 21,475. All in all a very healthy set of sales figures, which reflects the quality of the design of ADO16 and its popularity with the buying public.

Dean Oakey's Morris 1300 shows off its clean Pininfarina-styled lines, complemented by the very '70s Limeflower paint.

Chapter 2

Design, development and build

Introduction

The ADO16 was made in great numbers between 1962 and 1974, and was the most successful car produced on the home market during this time. The car was available in three body styles: a four-door saloon, a two-door saloon, and a three-door estate.

While the two- and four-door saloons were both introduced in 1962, initial deliveries of the two-door went to the export market, with the majority being built as MG

The passenger cabin of ADO16 was roomy enough for four or even five adults. The brochures emphasised this by showing the car with no doors.

models, leaving only the four-door Morris and MG models available to UK customers. The two-door eventually crept onto the home market in 1967, although the factory production figures do not distinguish between two- and four-door saloons from this date. The three-door estate versions were introduced in 1966, and were badged as either the Morris Traveller or the Austin Countryman, and produced in 1100 or 1300 forms until 1970, when the 1100cc version was dropped and the Countryman and Traveller versions were sold simply as the Austin or Morris 1300 Estate.

The ADO16 range embraced BMC's badge engineering policy with alacrity and enthusiasm, and the range was introduced in 1962 with Morris and MG models, rapidly followed by the Austin badged cars in 1963. The super luxury Vanden Plas Princess model was introduced in 1964, and the sporting and luxury (but not as luxurious as the Vanden Plas) Riley and Wolseley models were added in 1965.

The six-model range neatly covered all the bases, providing a wide choice of trim levels, ranging from utilitarian through sporty and up to luxurious, as well as appealing to the small number of diehard marque fanatics.

When the MG version of ADO16 was announced, it was justifiably touted as the most advanced MG ever. Its performance and practicality were probably unique at the time. Initially, only the export markets (mainly the US) got the two-door model, hence the left-hand drive shown on this early brochure.

ADO16 development teams

Two men were behind the initial design of ADO16: Alex Issigonis, BMC's chief designer who designed the car's layout and bodyshell with its extremely spacious interior; and Alex Moulton, who was responsible for the interconnected fluid and rubber sprung suspension that gave ADO16 its superb ride. A

third person behind the success of ADO16 was BMC engineer and Technical Manager Charles Griffin. It was he who led the team that brought ADO16 to production reality.

Design of ADO16 began in 1958 as one element of the BMC plan to update its model range: ADO15 (the Mini); ADO16 (the 1100); and ADO17 (the 1800 'Landcrab'). In order to achieve this plan, BMC also embarked on the expansion of its physical infrastructure to provide new or refurbished factory space for the production of the three new cars.

These are two of the many talented people who made ADO16 such a success. To the right is Alex Issigonis, who designed the car, and to the left is BMC Technical Manager, engineer Charles Griffon, who got the car into production.

Key to the design of all three cars was the aim to have a transverse engine with its gearbox in the sump, front-wheel drive, and a wheel at each corner to achieve the maximum amount of interior space for a given size of car. In order to get ADO16 to production there were two teams under Griffin: one taking on the body design, the other the chassis.

Reg Job and Alan Parker were responsible for the body design, taking into account the Pininfarina styling and the need to have a monocoque capable of meeting the interior space requirements while accommodating all of the technical requirements.

Chassis design was done by Alan Webb and Bob Shirley, and covered the installation of the engine, gearbox, cooling system and exhaust, front and rear subframes, Hydrolastic suspension units, steering rack and column, brakes, and, finally, the installation of the fuel tank and spare wheel.

Model developments

Introduction

The ADO16 range was treated to two updates over its production run, with the Mark II introduced in 1967 and the Mark III unveiled in 1971. The changes introduced at these points were evolutionary rather than revolutionary; changes to the basic body shape were minimal, as were mechanical modifications.

With Teal Blue paintwork, John Norris' 1300GT is a lovely example of the last model introduced. Only in production for a few years, the 1300GT was a fitting swansong for the performance versions of ADO16.

The Mark I models

Introduced in 1962, and retrospectively called the Mark I models, the range initially comprised the Morris two- and four-door saloons introduced in August that year, along with the four-door MG 1100, first on the market in October. One distinguishing feature of the Mark I Morris saloon was the

The Morris 1100 was the first model to be produced. A distinguishing mark is the chrome strip on the bonnet centreline, which did not appear on any other version of the car.

augmented by the Austin model in four-door saloon form in September 1963; the Vanden Plas Princess, first seen at the 1963 London Motor Show and put into production during 1964; the sporting Riley Kestrel and luxury sporting Wolseley in September 1965; and the three-door estate in Morris Traveller and Austin Countryman guise in March 1966. The main difference between the Morris and Austin 1100 was the interior, with the Austin being fitted with a strip speedometer rather than the central console on the Morris, which was also used on the MG 1100.

chromed strip mounted on the bonnet and running from the round Morris badge back to the scuttle.

By the introduction of the Mark II models the range had been

The MG version of ADO16 shared its strip speedometer with the Austin models. The MG had a bit more luxury in the form of wood trim on the dash, while the Austin had to make do with bare metal.

The Mark II models

Announced in October 1967, the changes that defined the Mark II models covered the complete range: the Austin and Morris two- and four-door saloons and estates (Countryman and

By 1969 the Mark II range was out. These three Morris versions show the two- and four-door saloons and the Traveler, replete with its fake wood trim. The inserts show the dashboards available with the strip speedometer for the Super De-luxe or the central console for the De-luxe models.

Traveller), as well as the MG, the Riley Kestrel, the Vanden Plas and the Wolseley.

The main change to the exterior of all models was quite subtle – the tops of the rear fins were cut away at an angle, so new rear light clusters were required, and these were angled forwards and the top length of the fin reduced. While the

The only significant styling change made to the body of ADO16 was the shortening of the rear fins with the introduction of the Mark II model. This resulted in the rear lights sloping forwards, as seen on this Mark III example Morris two-door saloon.

The interior of the Mark II Morris De-luxe had a circular speedometer mounted in a central binnacle with a wood surround.

original rear lights were almost vertical, the top of the rear of the wing fin was cut away so the new lights sloped forwards, giving a slightly sleeker look to the car's profile. The Morris saloon versions also lost the chrome bonnet strip, and all models gained a suspended headliner, replacing the glued-in-position item used in the Mark I models.

In 1969 the Riley model was replaced with the Austin and Morris 1300GT. This new addition to the sporting stable was powered by the twin-carburettor engine seen in the Riley 1300, and came in four-door form only.

The Mark III models

Announced in September 1971, the Mark III saloon range comprised the Austin 1100 and 1300 two- and four-door saloons, with the 1100 two-door saloon available in 'De-luxe' trim only, and the other three saloons in 'Super De-luxe' trim. By this time the Morris saloon versions had been discontinued in the home market, replaced by the Morris Marina. The other models in the range were the Austin and Morris 1300GT, Austin 1300 Countryman, Morris 1300 Traveller, Wolseley 1300 and Vanden Plas Princess 1300. There were no technical changes

The Austin Mark III range comprised the two- and four-door saloons and the estate Countryman, and were powered by either the 1100 or 1300 engines.

to the cars, with the changes being limited to 'improved luxury and durability'.

Externally, the Austins got a new matt black grille, with a single horizontal chrome bar on the 'De-luxe' trim level and three on the Super De-luxe models, along with what was described as 'modern' badging front and rear. In the name of safety, flush rectangular interior door handles were fitted, replacing the levers used in the Mark II.

It was the interior that received the most attention – the Super De-luxe seats were new and improved, wider than before, and had horizontal pleats; the rears were re-covered to match. There was a simulated wood grain dashboard running the full width of the interior, with a glovebox with lid opposite the passenger, plus face level fresh air vents at each end. The window frames in the doors were fitted with stainless steel trims, and the doors were fitted with armrests. The two-door 1300 had opening rear windows and passenger armrests on the rear panel. Finally, the Super De-luxe had deep pile carpeting fitted throughout.

The 'De-luxe' trim level did not have the full width dash, but had a Mark II style centre console housing the speedometer, which incorporated the fuel gauge, and the lights and wiper switches, and the floors were covered by rubber mats.

With the Riley having been dropped in July 1969, and the MG in September 1971, the remaining Mark III models were the MG, Vanden Plas and Wolseley models. The Vanden Plas gained larger foot pedals and the new moulded plastic surround for the heater controls, and these also featured on the Wolseley model,

Austin's Mark III Super De-luxe trim featured a full-width wooden dash with a pair of circular instruments.

Below: In the lower De-luxe trim level, Austins made do with a central binnacle with a single large-diameter speedometer that incorporated the fuel gauge.

along with new front door pockets, smaller sun visors, and new carpets with a deeper pile.

The design team

The design of ADO16 commenced during 1958 after the Mini's layout had been completed, and was to be a car to replace the Morris Minor in the BMC lineup. The design and development of ADO16 was overseen by BMC's Chief Engineer, Passenger Cars, Charles Griffin. Based at the Morris Motors works in Cowley, near Oxford, the project looked at a larger version of the Mini, and the scope of the project soon extended to make a car to replace the Austin A40 and the Riley and Wolseley 1500 as well as the Minor.

Because he was based in Austin's Longbridge plant and only

spent one day a week at Morris' Cowley plant, Issigonis had less input into the engineering design. This also meant that Griffin was equal in status to Issigonis so could (and did) have a lot more influence over the design.

The styling – Pininfarina

The styling of ADO16 was handed over to Italian car design house Pininfarina. At first sight this seems to be an odd decision, especially bearing in mind that the Mini, which was styled in-house by Alec Issigonis, was seen as a great example of form following function. The Mini's styling was roundly approved by all, but its simple two-box design was considered by many to be very stark. However, while the Mini was aimed at the bottom end of the market, as well as (probably accidentally) appealing to the 'trendy' and youth segments, ADO16 was aimed at a very different market sector.

The thinking behind the styling of ADO16 was to make the car appeal to the upper strata of the target market: the mature, family oriented, probably serious professionals who wanted a car that would fulfil their immediate needs of economical and reliable family transport but, all things being equal, would also be swayed in favour of a stylish and modern car in terms of both looks and what was under the skin.

So, with Pininfarina already having styled the A40 and the Austin Cambridge/Morris Oxford under its trademark Farina badge, it was a forgone conclusion that the Italians would get to style such an important car as ADO16.

They did not start from a clean sheet, however, as

A bucolic scene from the Mark I Austin brochure depicting the lifestyle of a typical 1100-owning family.

development of the new bodyshell was well in hand, and the basic shell was designed by Reg Job at Cowley. So Pininfarina had to work to a fairly constrained brief, with BMC sending measurements for all the elements of the car, including wheelbase, scuttle height, engine and gearbox, front and rear overhangs, and even the profile of the car. What's more, the design had to take into account Issigonis' need for the maximum amount of interior space that could be squeezed out of the design.

The project was led by Sergio Pininfarina, son of company

While ADO16 did not appear to have much of a boot, looks were deceptive and the actual boot volume was good.

and tyres made from sheet steel, as the requisite 12-inch wheels and tyres were not available. The mock-up showed up some problems with undercuts on the front and rear screens, which would have been hard (if not impossible) to manufacture, and an un-aerodynamic front end, both of which issues needed to be redesigned. Despite the constraints imposed by BMC and the problems with the first mock-up, Pininfarina came up with a modern, attractive and practical design, and also had a fair amount of influence on the interior, which was a lot less austere than the Mini.

The styling of ADO16's body was completed by 1959, and in the end there were only a couple of minor changes needed to

founder Battista, and a talented designer in his own right, and involved numerous visits from BMC designers, including Issigonis, to oversee progress and iron out any problems. Pininfarina's first attempt was a mock-up that even had wheels

Fitting the A-series engine in the nose of ADO16 was a masterpiece of packaging. This is a Mark I Morris 1100 engine bay with its single-carburettor.

the Pininfarina design to get the car into production. The rear of the Pininfarina-designed body was widened by around four inches, and curved side glass was introduced to give adequate room for three abreast seating on the rear bench seat. The front was also widened by around three inches to give more shoulder room, to allow for the curved glass, and to preserve the design's integrity.

The design and development process and timescales

Starting in 1958, the design process was long and complex, and involved many teams of talented engineers and designers.

Having designed and put the Mini into production, Issigonis was not content to just scale it up to make ADO16, but explored a number of options for the new car.

One concern was the loss of legroom in the front due to the

Despite the transverse engine and the design team's fears that it would limit front legroom, ADO16's front seats give more than adequate room for even the longest of legs. This is Jim Hills' MG Mark I.

The clever Hydrolastic suspension used rubber springing, and the displacement units were linked front-to-back to control body movement.

fitment of a transverse engine, but positioning the gearbox below the engine helped to alleviate that issue.

There is a sketch by Issigonis held by the BMIHT at Gaydon that showed his early thoughts about the mechanical layout of ADO16 – all contained within a body shape that is recognisably ADO16's Pininfarina-styled body. There are four different layouts – the top being a front-wheel drive transverse A-series with Hydrolastic suspension; second a rear-wheel drive with a longitudinally mounted B-series engine and conventional suspension; the third the longitudinal B-series with conventional suspension; and finally, the transverse A-series with conventional suspension.

The standout innovation adopted by ADO16 was its Hydrolastic suspension system, with each side linked together, which was unlike any setup previously used worldwide. The suspension had been under development since 1956, with Issigonis and Moulton experimenting with Morris 1000s fitted with various iterations of the system. It was the design of ADO16 that gave Issigonis the impetus to finish the setup, and, in interviews in *The Motor*, Griffin reveals that he and BMC Engineering Director George Harriman had to pressure Issigonis to incorporate the system into ADO16.

Prototype subframes were made by Pressed Steel under the supervision of Harry Barber, and the prototype cars were built at Cowley. The prototype build program resulted in an initial 12 prototype cars being produced and road tested during 1960, with a further 12 improved prototypes built and tested during 1961, before the design was finalised for production.

The last model produced for the ADO16 range was the 1300GT. Available in both Austin and Morris badging, this is John Norris' Morris version.

at Longbridge, although the automatic gearboxes were built at the Kings Norton plant from components from Automotive Products (AP). The front and rear subframes and various other components, such as the instruments, were bought in from various suppliers, mostly UK based. The seats and trim were produced at Longbridge and Cowley, and the non-standard luxury trim needed for the Vanden Plas model was produced at Vanden Plas' London works.

To produce ADO16 in the numbers required, BMC set up two production lines at Longbridge, and another two at Cowley, increasing production capacity to over 7000 ADO16s per day. At Longbridge the all new CAB (Car Assembly Building) No 2 was built in 1962 expressly to produce ADO16 in saloon form. Later, production of the 1100 estate (as well as a small number of saloons) was carried out at CAB No 1 alongside the Mini.

The Vanden Plas variant was finished at the Vanden Plas London Works works after the basic car was assembled. Initially Longbridge-built cars were used, but later on in production Cowley-built models were used.

Into production

The bodyshells for ADO16 were produced from the basic pressings at five plants within BMC:

• Nuffield Metal Products, Birmingham
• Pressed Steel at Cowley
• Pressed Steel at Swindon
• Austin at Longbridge
• Fisher and Ludlow at Castle Bromwich, Birmingham

Various plants were used to produce the major components of ADO16, all of which fed into the final assembly lines at Longbridge and Cowley.

All the engine and transmission units were produced

Above: Roy Robinson's Morris Traveller is a Mark II version, and Roy has owned it since 2021. It is a rare survivor, having never been restored, only maintained fastidiously over its life.

Right: The Traveller had fake wood panels in a nod to the then-current styling trends, and the roofline is extended when compared to the saloons.

Owners' impressions

Roy Robinson's Traveller

Roy Robinson owns a rather nice Morris Traveller Mark II from 1971 painted in the rare Aqua colour, with Navy interior. Roy has owned the car since March 2022, but has known it for many years and always secretly wanted it! When the previous owner, Pauline Cleary, a much loved member of the 1100 Club gave up driving, her family turned to the Club to find a new custodian, and Roy was the lucky fellow chosen to be the new owner. The car had been known to the Club for over 20 years, and was a regular at many Club meetings, and the family wanted the new owner to continue to use the car in Club events as well as driving it regularly.

When Roy acquired the car it was in very good condition,

Above: The Traveller's rear hatch was a bit of a novelty at the time, giving unrivalled access to a roomy load area. The rear seats could be folded to provide a carpeted load area or reversed to sit with their cushions up, so, with the front seats reclined, they could form a double bed.

Right: The current custodian of the Morris Traveller, Roy Robinson.

with a current MOT and recent service, and since then Roy has been, as he put it, 'future proofing' it – making sure that the car will be in better shape in ten years' time than it is today. To that end he has been 'correcting' some areas of the body, to return them to an as original condition, and the brakes have been thoroughly overhauled and the suspension units on the off-side have been replaced.

The car's very neat interior has not been neglected, with a new carpet set installed and a small repair made to the driver's seat vinyl. Future plans include fitting a new rear subframe; Roy has sourced a new old stock item and is just waiting for a chance to fit it. Once in situ he will also refit missing parts of the tow bar – while the car was with the Cleary family it would often tow a trailer on family holidays – and Roy intends to tow an early '70s Sprite caravan!

Importantly, Roy has the full history of the car. As a virtually one-family-car-from-new, the comprehensive history details all the jobs needed to keep the car running and in tip top condition. Roy is continuing this history, adding to it as he keeps improving the car. This is important, as the car has an unbroken record of being on the road and used – it has always been a family car and has had everything needed to maintain it as an everyday runner in great condition.

Roy loves the car, and his personal history also contains quite a few ADO16s – starting with his parents who had an Austin 1300 in 1974, and he has owned 1300s virtually his entire driving life, with his first car being a Traveller like his current one.

It helped, of course, that, originally based in Oxford, many of Roy's family members worked for BMC and British Leyland, so brand loyalty was bred into Roy from an early age. Roy loves his new Traveller and reckons that the best thing about he car is the history and rarity – the comprehensive record of the car's life is probably unique and underlines just how important the car is – both to Roy as the current custodian, the Club as a well known and much loved example of the breed, and for the classic car movement as a whole.

Such cars may not be multi-cylindered exotic Grand Tourers with a competition history and a string of illustrious owners, but it's cars like Roy's that form the bedrock of the classic car movement, and they are the sort of cars that will be remembered and still be on the road when the exotics can only be seen in a museum.

www.veloce.co.uk / www.velocebooks.com
All current books • New book news • Special offers • Gift vouchers

Chapter 3
The oily bits

Introduction

ADO16 was a neat design that could legitimately be called a grown up Mini, with both cars sharing the overall mechanical layout. With its space-saving transverse engine with gearbox in the sump, unitary/monocoque bodyshell and Hydrolastic suspension, the 1100/1300 car was right at the cutting edge of current technology. It was well designed and built, and was reliable, robust and comfortable – traits that were reflected in the model's popularity and sales.

The bodyshell

ADO16 continued with the innovative design and engineering first seen in the Mini, the brainchild of engineering genius Alec Issigonis. ADO16's passengers were carried in a small and rigid monocoque shell, and the mechanical parts were all carried on separate subframes that were isolated from the main monocoque structure using metalastic bushes – effectively placing a layer of rubber between the subframe and the shell, and isolating the passengers from the mechanical components and the road. This meant that the passenger cell was insulated from both road and mechanical noise and vibration, giving the car a very refined feel.

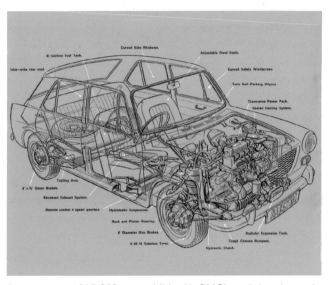

This cutaway of ADO16 was published in BMC's early brochures. It gives an excellent view of the anatomy of the car.

The bodyshell originally came in two- or four-door form with a conventional boot; a three-door Traveller/Countryman estate version that incorporated a hatchback rear door was added after production commenced. The shell was based

This cutaway skeleton of an actual Traveller is now owned by the 1100 Club. This view gives a good idea of the excellent interior space of the car.

At the front, the 1100 cutaway shows the engine installation. Note the position of the front Hydrolastic unit just behind the radiator, and the grille in the inner wing panel to allow air to flow through the radiator.

around its floorpan, with the strength of the structure given by the box section sills running along each side, and the open 'transmission' tunnel down the centre of the floor.

The floorpan was braced transversely by three structures: the dash assembly at the front, which also supported the front wheelarches, and a pair of box sections. The first of these ran transversely across the centre of the cabin, and also provided

the front mounting points for the front seats, and the second ran across the car below the rear bulkhead.

In the boot, a panel, which included wells for the spare wheel and the fuel tank, tied together the rear inner wings and provided the rear mounting points for the rear subframe. The sides and roof panels were welded to this base structure to form a rigid and stiff shell. Thanks to its longer doors, the three-door body's 'B' pillar was slightly further back than that on the four-door, while the Traveller/Countryman estate used the three-door saloon body with the same wheelbase as the saloon, but had an extended roofline to accommodate the rear hatch.

The only issue that arose with the bodyshell, apart from the inevitable rust, was found in early cars, which could suffer from problems with the sill strength when the jack was used. The use of the early jack could crush the sill structure around the jacking points, and so this was quickly fixed by beefing up the jacking points and changing the jack design. The mechanical elements of the car were mounted on separate subframes, one front and one rear. The front and rear subframes were fabricated from pressed steel sheet, and both were fitted to the main shell with four mounts on the rear and six on the front.

The subframe mounts were designed to use the rubber element of the mount in sheer, and allowed limited movement of the complete subframe in relation to the bodyshell to be a maximum of 0.10in (0.254cm) while insulating the main shell from noise and vibration generated by the road wheels and the mechanical elements of the car.

The bodyshell of ADO16 was state of the art in 1962 and, thanks to the experience the company had in designing the Mini, threw up few problems, although the shell does harbour some rust traps. The basic structure and the car's styling remained largely unchanged throughout the model's life,

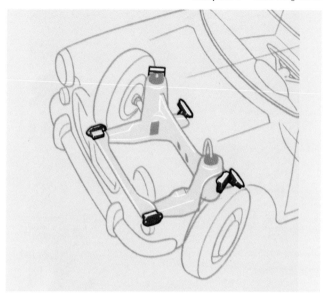

The front subframe was mounted to the bodyshell using six rubber mounts designed to isolate the body from the mechanical components while minimising the movement of the subframe.

except for minor updates to the rear wings, showing just how right the design was from the word go.

The engine
Introduction
Throughout the life of ADO16 the cars were fitted with either

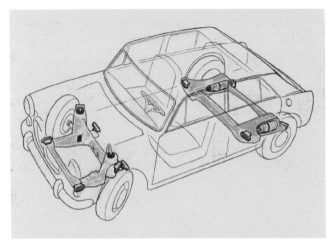

The two subframes are seen here. Four mounts were used on the rear subframe.

The engine was a tight fit in the shell, sitting between the two front Hydrolastic units and mounted onto the front subframe; it was a masterpiece of packaging. Note the long gearbox extension running backward to position the gearlever in the cabin.

the 1098cc or 1275cc versions of BMC's A-series engine. The design of the A-series engine was started in 1949 by Austin and was initially named the AS3, although it was quickly renamed as the A-series. Mooted as a very small engine to slot into the range below the larger B-series unit and replacing the venerable Austin 7 engine, the A-series was a four-cylinder, overhead valve unit with initially a capacity of a mere 803cc, and was first fitted to the new A30 model in 1951. The 1275cc version was the largest production version produced by BMC.

The A-series and the RAC tax formula

Although the A-series engine was initially produced in 1953 it was still reasonably modern by the time it was used in ADO16, and while it had a longer stroke than bore design, luckily the influence of the 'RAC' power formula used to determine the UK tax rating of cars in the pre- and early post-war eras had waned by the time of its design, leaving it a lot less compromised than some other units.

Here is an example of the A-series engine in its original longitudinal configuration. In this case, it is in a Mark I MG Midget where access is a little better than it is in ADO16.

The RAC system calculated a notional power for an engine, and up to the 1940s the formula was used to define the taxation class of a vehicle – hence the pre-war names of cars such as the Austin 7 or Morris 12 – the number representing the car's taxation class as RAC formula horsepower. The higher the class, the greater the cost of the yearly 'Road Fund Licence' or road tax, and in the UK this tax was a significant yearly cost in the running of a car.

The RAC formula was calculated thus: (DxDxN)/2.5 where 'D' is the cylinder bore, and 'N' is the number of cylinders. The formula made no consideration of the engine capacity or the actual power produced, and meant that an engine with a small bore and long stroke would be taxed less than an engine of the same capacity but with a larger bore and shorter stroke.

The tax formula influenced British car designers of the '20s, '30s and '40s to produce long-stroke engines that tended to produce more torque but less power – a configuration that was a good match to the UK's 'rolling English roads' but not a formula that produced high revs or high power.

While the car tax system was overhauled after World War Two, dumping the RAC formula, it had still had some residual influence over the design of the A-series engine as this was what engine designers were experienced in.

There were two main downsides to a long-stroke or over-square engine. The first was the relatively narrow bores gave less room to fit the valves, meaning smaller valves and, therefore, compromised breathing. The second was to limit the revs of the engine – the piston speed of a long-stroke engine will always be faster than that of a short-stroke engine, and this means there are greater loads on the long-stroke engine as the piston changes direction at the top and bottom of each stroke. Despite these negatives, and while the A-series engine was neither the most powerful nor the most advanced engine of the day, it was a reliable, robust unit and produced the right mixture of power and torque to happily propel ADO16 down the typical twisty roads of the UK.

The A-series development for ADO16

Prior to the introduction of ADO16, the A-series engine had powered the conventional front-engined, rear-drive small Austins and Morris models, including the Morris Minor and Austin A30/40, and Austin Healy 'Frogeye' Sprite in capacities of 803cc and 948cc. The Mini and the 1100 needed the transverse A-series engine with its in-sump gearbox, and this unit had been produced for the Mini in a new 848cc capacity thanks to it using a 948cc block but with a shortened stroke of 68.26mm combined with the standard bore of 62.9mm.

This new version worked well in the Mini, but the 1100 would need more power and torque to cater for its larger size, weight and carrying capacity, so the engine capacity was raised to 1098cc by increasing the bore and stroke to 64.58 and 83.72mm respectively. This increased capacity was combined with a new cylinder head (the 12G202 first seen on the 997cc Mini Cooper in 1961) which had larger inlet valves and ports.

Two views of the MG unit crammed into Jim Hills' very original Mark I MG 1100. While the twin-carburettors are a tight fit between the engine and the bulkhead, there is actually a reasonable amount of room at the front of the engine to access the ignition system, fan belt, dynamo, and clutch slave cylinder for servicing.

While this may seem straightforward, the actual process was somewhat fraught, as the original 803cc engine had not been designed with the prospect of such a large increase in capacity in mind. Going up to 948cc had resulted in the cylinder bores being paired, or 'siamesed', resulting in little 'meat' between each pair of bores, but luckily the inherent strength of the block meant that there was just enough metal to allow the increase in the bore size while retaining the existing block. This new version of the A-series gave 48bhp at 5100rpm, while torque was a healthy 60ftlb at 2500rpm, and was perfect for ADO16.

In this new 1098cc form the A-series also went on to power many more Austin and Morris cars, including the A35 van, A40, Minis, Minors, MG Midget and the Austin Healey Sprite.

The first change to the 1100's engine occurred just after the range was launched, when the MG 1100 engine used a new cylinder head design, designated 12G295. This had changes to the combustion chambers, which, along with twin SU carburettors gave a 7bhp power boost, up to 55bhp at 5500rpm.

The A-series engine in ADO16
The 1100's 'A' engines followed the usual format for British car engines during the 1960s – it was a was a straight four, with pushrod operated overhead valves, two valves per cylinder, cast iron crankcase and cylinder head, and a forged steel crankshaft with three main bearings. The main and big end bearings were split shell type.

The valves were sited vertically in line in the cylinder head, which had kidney-shaped combustion chambers, while the inlet and exhaust ports were sited on the same side of the head. This layout had four individual inlet ports and three exhaust ports, as the centre two cylinders' exhaust ports were 'siamesed' in the head casting. The ports were sited on the back of the head when viewed from the front of the car. The valves were operated by rockers mounted on a single rocker shaft on the top of the head, which was carried on five bolt-on pedestals. A pressed steel rocker cover covered the valves, and incorporated the engine breather pipework and the oil filler cap. The valve adjustment was carried out by screw and locknut on the pushrod side of the rocker.

The cylinder head was a type 12G202 (the number is cast in between the rocker pedestals) and was the same as that used on the 998cc Mini Cooper engine. However the early MG version was fitted with the 12G206 head, which had improved porting and double valve springs; this head was also fitted to the Wolseley and Riley engines. From 1965, the MG, Riley and Wolseley heads were 12G295 types, with larger inlet ports and revised exhaust porting.

The pushrods were operated from the camshaft, which was mounted in the block on the manifold side, and was carried on shell bearings. The camshaft was driven by a short timing chain from the nose of the crankshaft, which was housed under a pressed steel timing cover. The oil pump was mounted at the flywheel end of the motor, and was driven from the end of the camshaft. It fed oil into a gallery where it was routed into the crankshaft via the three main bearings, and from there drillings took it to the big end bearings. The gallery was also drilled to feed oil to the camshaft bearings.

Oil was also directed, via drillings in the block, up to the head, where it lubricated the rocker shaft. The oil system incorporated a differential oil pressure switch in the filter assembly. This measured the difference in pressure between the feed inlet and output sides, it would illuminate the oil pressure warning light when the filter was becoming clogged – apparently this could take only around 3000 miles at which point a filter change was needed. Cooling was taken care of with a water pump mounted on the front of the engine, driven from the fanbelt. Water temperature was thermostatically controlled, with the thermostat mounted on the right-hand side of the head and covered by an alloy casting to which was fitted the top hose that led directly to the top of the radiator.

The 1300 engine was very similar to the 1100. However, after the problems BMC had with increasing the capacity of the 948cc unit to create the 1100, it was no surprise that there would need to be even more juggling of the engine's layout to increase the size further.

The 1300 engine actually displaced 1275cc, and came about

In the original MG brochure, the engine bay is pretty well laid out and very similar to the actual examples.

thanks to the development of the Mini Cooper S. The first Cooper S engine had an undersquare 970cc engine with a bore and stroke of 70.6mm x 61.9mm, and shared its block with the existing 948cc unit, which left very little scope for rebores. The second Cooper S engine was a 1071cc unit that had modified bore centres to allow for the larger bores. While it retained

The radiator had a steel cowling around it to funnel air through it. The thermostat was mounted on the end of the cylinder head.

John Norris' Morris 1300GT engine bay sports the trademark twin-carburettors of a sporting ADO16. It also has a quickly detachable cover over the front of the engine, which was intended to protect the ignition system from rainwater and spray. Note also the servo behind the battery to give the brakes a boost.

the bore of 70.6mm, the stroke was increased to 68.26mm. In addition, the cylinder head had an extra stud added at the thermostat end of the block to provide better clamping of the head gasket. The cylinder block was also slightly deeper than the original.

The 1275cc version of the Cooper S was a long-stroke version of the new 1071cc unit, and, thanks to the revised bore spacings, had a bore and stroke of 70.6mm by 81.3mm. It was this unit that formed the basis for that fitted to the 1300 versions of ADO16, and was used across the range in various states of tune.

The cooling system used in ADO16 was similar to that of the Mini, with the radiator mounted on the nearside of the engine bay. The belt-driven multi-blade fan was positioned in a metal cowl on the inside edge of the radiator, and, on the outer edge, there was a second steel cowl that directed the hot air into vents pressed into the inner wing panel and allowed the hot air to be expelled into the wheelarch. This is one reason that the left-hand wings on ADO16 (and the Mini) tend not to rust as much as the right-hand wings, as the hot air helped to dry out

In contrast, Dean Oakey's 'cooking' Morris 1300 does not have the rain cover or servo, and sports a single-carburettor with a 'wrap-around' air filter. Its radiator cowl is missing.

mud and road debris thrown up by the wheel and caught under the wing. The thermostat sat on the nearside of the cylinder head, and its housing carried the water to the top of the radiator via a hose. The one weak spot of the cooling system was the notorious external bypass hose that connected water passages in the head to the block. If the hose failed then it was potentially a head-off job to fix.

The heating and ventilation system used a separate heater matrix, mounted in the heater box inside the cabin.

Summary: The A-series engine in ADO16
The A-series engine was an ideal fit for ADO16. It was tough, reliable and refined, its few weaknesses having been ironed out over several years of production prior to ADO16's introduction. In ADO16 it gave plenty of power, but, more importantly in a family car, plenty of torque. Its flexible nature suited ADO16 down to the ground, giving the car more than adequate performance, and its simple mechanical makeup meant it was easy and cheap to maintain. It was an eager and willing power plant and its friendly character at the heart of ADO16 was a major factor in the car's success.

The transmission
Introduction
There were two transmission options for the ADO16 range: manual or automatic, and both came with four forward and one reverse gear. The first cars came with the manual gearbox only, and the automatic was introduced in 1965 as an option on ADO16 as well as the Mini. The automatic transmission was a new and innovative design that allowed the driver to treat the drive either as a pure automatic or use the gearlever to manually change gears without having to use a clutch.

ADO16 manual transmission
The manual car's clutch was a single-plate unit, with the clutch diaphragm spring assembly mounted on the outside of the

The interior of Dean Oakey's Morris 1300 shows the under-dash shelf featured on all the cars in the range, and was a useful oddments space. The short gearlever of the manual four-speed box is sensibly positioned in the centre of the car.

flywheel, and the clutch plate with its drive splines and the pressure plate mounted on the inboard side of the flywheel – sandwiching the flywheel between the two assemblies. The diaphragm was bolted to the flywheel and the pressure plate, and pulled the pressure plate towards the flywheel to engage the clutch. The clutch was disengaged via a thrust bearing fitted on the outside edge of the diaphragm, and operated by the clutch hydraulic slave cylinder via a lever on the outside of the engine casing.

Power was fed from the clutch plate via a train of three drop gears down to the gearbox main shaft in the sump. The gears were mounted inboard of the clutch, with the top drop gear running on a sleeve concentric with the outside of the crankshaft end. This gear was driven from the splines on the clutch plate, the middle drop gear was, in effect, an idler, and was mounted on a short shaft below the crank line. The final drop gear was mounted on the gearbox main shaft to drive the gearbox.

The manual gearbox offered four forward and one reverse gear, and was of conventional design with a main and layshafts carrying the gears, and each selected gear depending on the relevant gear cog being locked in place by selector forks operated by rods from the remote gearlever. The four-speed and reverse unit used baulk ring synchromesh on second, third and top gears. First gear did not receive synchromesh until 1969.

The most unusual feature of the gearbox was the fact that it lived underneath the A-series engine in a cast aluminium sump, and shared its oil with the engine. When this layout first appeared in the Mini in 1959, the naysayers believed that the lack of specific gear oil as used in conventional gearboxes of the time would result in a short life. However, as time has shown, this was not the case – BMC designed the gearbox to run in conventional engine oil, and the relatively frequent engine oil changes needed by both the Mini and ADO16 resulted in the gearbox, in manual or automatic guise, getting new oil regularly. This made the gearbox one of the most reliable components in the car, with the gearbox oil being renewed at every service!

The differential was incorporated in the transmission casing, and was a conventional but compact planet and sun unit; much the same as that used on the Mini, but with a drive ratio of 4.13:1. The inner ends of the drive shafts were fitted to the transmission using Moulton elastic universal joints, made from forged steel spiders, to which cone-shaped rubber bushes encased in a steel cover were bonded. These rubber bushes were fixed to the forked ends of the shaft using 'U' bolts. The use of rubber added a certain amount of cushioning to the transmission.

These rubber bushes can fail if they become soaked in oil, for example if the gearbox output shaft seals have failed or if there's a persistent engine oil leak.

ADP16 automatic transmission
The automatic gearbox was designed by AP (Automotive Products) of Leamington Spa, and was the culmination of some ten years' research into an automatic gearbox for a small car.

While the automatic gearbox was placed in the sump of the A-series engine, just like the manual, the sump casting was slightly larger, and, like the manual, shared its oil with the engine. Just as with the manual box, the use of the engine oil was included in the design brief, so caused no problems in operation.

A rotary hydraulic torque converter, described by BMC as a 'Hydrokinetic unit,' replaced the manual unit's clutch and flywheel assembly, and sent the power to the gearbox input shaft using a train of three helical gears similar to the manual box system.

The power was directed to a main bevel gear train, housed in the gearbox, and which was described as a differential within a differential. The selection of actual gears relied on a combination of a sprag clutch, and hydraulically operated clutch bands and discs to hold or lock various parts of the bevel

The automatic gearbox was a compact unit and fitted in a slightly modified gearbox housing that made the unit slightly taller than the manual one. The clutch was replaced with a small torque converter (shown in red on this picture).

gear train in order to select the four individual forward and one reverse gears. The brake bands were used to select the four forward ratios, and two hydraulic clutches were employed: one to provide all four forward gears, the second was used either to supplement fourth gear or to provide reverse. The bands and clutches were operated by valves in the hydraulic system, and the valves were controlled by cables operated from the gearchange lever in the cabin.

The hydraulic system used the engine oil, and was pressurised on startup by the engine's oil pump, while an auxiliary pump pressurised the system when the car was moving, thus allowing the car to be tow started if required.

Output from the gearbox was was by helical gear to a conventional differential and then drive shafts to the wheels, with a layout similar to the manual version. The box did not have a 'free-wheel' capability – when the throttle was released the engine remained 'attached' to the road wheels through the gearbox, thus providing engine braking.

One of the selling points of the automatic transmission was that it could be operated either in fully automatic or manual modes. The gearchange lever allowed the driver to put the box in 'D' for Drive and the box would change automatically, or the driver could manually engage first, second, third or fourth gears (and reverse) manually, and the box would hold each gear – the driver could then change up or down just by moving the gearlever to the required ratio.

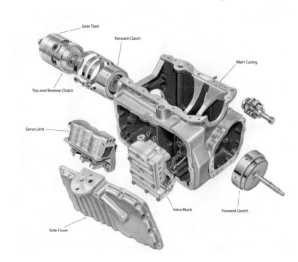

The major elements of the AP automatic gearbox.

The automatic gearbox sump or casing was slightly larger in volume than the manual version, which meant the automatic car's engine and transmission units sat slightly higher than the manual alternative. The extra height meant a small redesign of the front subframe and the use of an annular air filter, instead of the manual unit's high-mounted flat cleaner, to enable the unit to clear the standard bonnet.

To allow for power losses in the new transmission without affecting performance, automatic cars' engines were given a 10% power boost over the manual.

In order to produce the various components for the new gearbox in its plant in Leamington Spa, AP moved its 'Purolator' filter division to Bolton, and, in the vacated space, set up a new Automatic Gearbox Division. The new site produced the various components and sub-assemblies needed to build the gearboxes.

While AP produced most of the gearbox parts, BMC supplied the main sump and differential castings, bevel gear train, main shaft and oil pump. BMC assembled the automatic gearboxes at its Kings Norton plant in a clean room specifically designed for the purpose.

The automatic gearbox supplied by AP for ADO16 was an innovative and clever design that managed to combine the advantages of an automatic box (no clutch pedal) with those of a manual (manual selection of gears as required). It was a reliable and easy-to-use unit that enhanced the marketability of ADO16 (and the Mini), giving the car a real advantage over many of its rivals.

The suspension

Introduction

Designed by Issigonis, along with Dr Alex Moulton, the system used a combination of rubber springing and hydraulic fluid damping, which replaced the traditional steel springs and separate shock absorbers. ADO16 was the first car to use this design of suspension, and its introduction was largely trouble-

The automatic's gearlever was positioned on the floor between the front seats. It could be used either as a manual clutchless four-speed or as a true automatic.

free. The proof of the system was that it went on to be used across the BMC range.

The Hydrolastic system

The system relied on two factors: the progressive springing properties of rubber and the interaction between the front and rear suspension units using hydraulics. A Hydrolastic displacement unit was placed on each wheel, and on each side the front and rear units were connected together with flexible

This is the top of a Hydrolastic unit mounted in the front subframe. The hose allows the fluid to flow to and from the rear unit.

pipes that ran down the centre of the car below the cabin in the 'transmission' tunnel – note that there was no side-to-side linkage. Each displacement unit was made from two pressed steel parts: a steel top case and a lower spacer.

The casing had a moulded-in rubber spring, and at its top was a connector that allowed fluid to flow from and to its paired unit. The lower edge of the top casing was wrapped round to form an hydraulic seal with a pressed steel spacer, which had a bleed hole in its edge, and a number of larger ports in its top surface, giving the whole unit two interconnected chambers in which the hydraulic fluid was housed. The chamber below the lower spacer was sealed with a flexible nylon reinforced butyl rubber diaphragm. The diaphragm was fitted with a tapered piston that pushed or pulled against the diaphragm when the suspension moved. The top case was fixed to the car's chassis, and the tapered piston was fitted to the suspension using a load thrust button, so any suspension movement caused the piston to push or pull at the diaphragm.

The shape of the piston and its interaction with the diaphragm meant that the volume of the fluid displaced increased according to the distance travelled by the piston. When combined with the geometry of the suspension this gave a variable (rising) rate of suspension compliance as more movement was input.

Movement of the suspension moved the diaphragm, which, in turn, caused the fluid to compress the rubber spring in the

The Hydrolastic units on each side of the car were linked together by pipes to allow the transfer of fluid from front to rear.

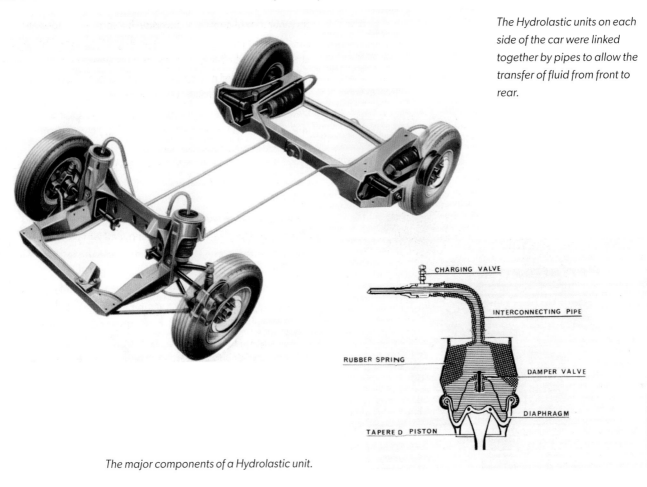

The major components of a Hydrolastic unit.

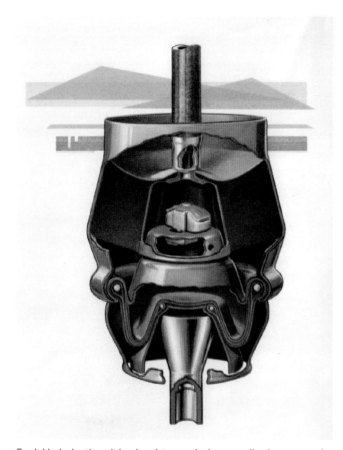

Each Hydrolastic unit had a piston on its base, a diaphragm, and two compartments containing fluid.

top chamber giving the suspension its 'spring' component. Damping was provided by the fluid moving between the two chambers via the bleed hole or the ports in the spacer.

With low wheel movements, typically at low speeds or on smooth roads, the fluid was displaced between the two chambers via the bleed hole in the spacer. When there was more suspension movement or a rapid shock, the larger ports in the spacer came into operation, allowing greater movement of fluid between the two chambers. These valves, which were sealed using flexible rubber flaps set up to only allow the valve to work when required, allowed fluid to travel from the lower chamber to the top chamber when the suspension compressed to give 'bump' damping, and when the suspension decompressed they allowed fluid to travel from the top to the lower chamber for 'rebound' damping.

The hydraulic fluid was 49% water, 49% methyl-alcohol as an anti freeze agent, 1% of a rust inhibitor and 1% of a distasteful dye. The dye was put in as a requirement of UK Customs and Excise to ensure no-one would be tempted to drink the mixture. Water was used rather than oil as water not only had constant viscosity throughout the system's operating temperatures, but it also was able to efficiently absorb and dissipate the heat generated by the system while it was in operation.

When a wheel was running on a bumpy surface the Hydrolastic unit on each wheel would be absorbing the road imperfections with the rubber spring, but would also have the

As the car's wheel was deflected by bumps in the road, the fluid was displaced from that corner's Hydrolastic unit to the other unit on that side, helping to keep the car level.

hydraulic fluid moving between the two linked Hydrolastic units to maintain the car's ride height.

The interaction between the front and rear units provided strong control of pitch (ie up and down movement) as the displacement of one wheel by a bump pushed the hydraulic fluid to the other unit. So, when the car hit a bump in the road, this would compress the front suspension but would also cause the nose to lift; however the fluid in the front Hydrolastic unit would be diverted to the rear unit, lifting it as well, so keeping the ride height level as well as counteracting the pitch. The system also gave the car good resistance to roll. When the car went round a corner, the connection between front and rear Hydrolastic units meant that the two interconnected units on the inside edge of the cornering car resisted the cornering forces trying to compress the suspension. This was because while the cornering forces tried to move both wheels up, this would attempt to compress the fluid in both units, but, as the fluid was incompressible and had nowhere to go, it meant that the suspension automatically stiffened, restricting wheel movement and hence reducing any roll. All in all the system was clever, simple and worked extremely well. It also had few moving parts to wear out or degrade over time.

As well as being very good from a functional perspective, providing the ADO16 with a compliant and reliable suspension system, the Hydrolastic system was also relatively cheap and easy to mass produce, albeit not as cheap as the all rubber

The various elements of the Hydrolastic suspension in situ: the subframes, the Hydrolastic units, and transfer pipes.

compounds, simplifying production and cutting down on the number of components needed. During the life of the unit on the car if there was any settling of the suspension due to the rubber 'creeping,' the correct hight could be regained by resetting the correct static hydraulic pressure.

springing seen on the first Minis. There was only one forging used in the system, the piston rod, while the rest of the metal components were made from simple steel pressings. Many of the pressings were designed to be complemented by the metal pressing techniques employed, such as the taper used on some pressings. There was no precision machining needed on any of the pressed steel components, and the metal components were cadmium plated to to extend their life. In production, the assembly of each unit did not require gaskets or sealing

The suspension

ADO16's front suspension followed the example set by the Mini, with the complete suspension system mounted on a subframe, and had single, unequal length, upper and lower links, with the lower link positioning controlled by a forward angled torque arm, which, in effect, was a radius arm or trailing link. The lower link (a steel forging) pivoted on a rubber bush.

At the wheel end the hub carrier was mounted on a simple swivel joint. The top link was a simple arm, and its inner end was mounted on the subframe by a pair of bearings in a fairly wide mounting. The Hydrolastic unit was fitted vertically in a turret above the top link's mounting, and the tapered piston was mounted on the arm close to the pivot by a suspension load thrust button that allowed the piston to be moved up and down as the pivot moved. The flexible pipe running to the rear unit exited from the top of the Hydrolastic unit.

At the wheel end, the top link was fixed to the hub carrier by a conventional swivel joint. The hub carrier was a substantial iron casting, and carried a stub axle on a pair of bearings. The drive shaft was articulated using a Birfield-Rzeppa constant velocity joint, and the the brake caliper was bolted to the front. The steering arm was bolted to the top of the hub carrier and went backwards to pick up the steering rack.

As with the front suspension, ADO16's rear suspension followed the lead of the Mini with a relatively simple trailing arm system, which, again, was mounted on a separate subframe. Mounted on the front edge of the rear subframe, the trailing arms were fabricated steel items, with a broad base to accommodate the pivot. The arms ran on a removable spindle, and were carried on a pair of adjustable taper roller bearings. At the other end of the arm was a small hub carrier that carried the brake drum, while the brake backplate was bolted directly to the arm. The Hydrolastic unit's tapered piston was fixed close to the pivot end of the arm using a load thrust button, and the unit itself was fitted horizontally onto the subframe at a

slight upwards angle. The hydraulic linking flexible hole exited towards the rear of the car, and the unit itself was bolted to, and enclosed top and bottom, by the subframe structure. As well as the Hydrolastic unit, the rear suspension also had an anti-roll bar fitted to join both trailing arms, and each trailing arm also had its own anti-pitch bar. The anti-pitch bar was a short torsion bar that had one end fitted to the inside edge of the trailing arm and the other end anchored on the front rail of the subframe. The anti-pitch bar was used to give some extra pitch control by effectively stiffening the springing when required.

Brakes

The hydraulic braking system featured Lockheed components, and used discs at the front and drums at the rear. Disc brakes were unusual on small cars at that time, and this was used extensively in the marketing material to promote the advanced design and technology included in the cars.

At the front the solid discs were 8in (20.32cm) in diameter, and the caliper was a twin opposed piston unit. The rear drums were also 8in (20.32cm) diameter with a width of 1¼in (3.175cm). There was just a single brake circuit, as was common at the time, and no servo assistance, although some export cars gained dual-circuit brakes in the mid 1960s, and servos started to appear around that time as well. The rear brake lines incorporated a pressure limiting valve to avoid rear wheel lockup under braking.

ADO16 sported disc brakes on the front – very rare for the time on family cars. Twin opposed-piston calipers gripped 8in diameter solid rotors.

The whole car demonstrated that the Mini concept could be scaled up to provide reliable and comfortable motoring to the masses, and the market agreed by buying the cars in their thousands.

Owners' impressions

David Haycock's Mark I Riley 1100

David Haycock, stalwart of the southern branch of the 1100 Club, owns a 1966 Riley Kestrel Mark I. David's liking for the 1100 started at a young age, when his father was stationed with the Royal Navy in Singapore and hired a Fiesta Yellow Morris 1100 while the family Triumph Herald Estate was being resprayed. David thought the 1100 was the bee's knees, and that impression stayed with him.

By 1987 David owned an Austin 1300 Mark II, and had joined the (then young) 1100/1300 Club. Thanks to the influence of the area organiser who owned a Mark I Vanden Plas, he decided to get himself a Mark I of some description. David points out that around this time when he started liking the ADO16; the cars were not really considered to be 'classics', and, in fact, it was the publication of a very downbeat buyer's guide article in the classic motoring press that led to the formation of the 1100

Conclusion

While ADO16 was largely based on the mechanical elements first seen on the Mini, its use of Hydrolastic suspension was the first time this innovative system was used in anger. The reliability of the Hydrolastic system and the superb ride and comfort that the system gave the car marked it out in market.

Club, as owners banded together to help preserve the much maligned model. The attitude towards the ADO16 in classic circles has now changed, and David is happy to see the cars are now perceived to be undoubted classics.

To scratch his itch for a Mark I, David uncovered a Riley 1100 in London, near Clapham Common, and reasonably close to where he lived on the south coast. It was a very original, three-owner car. The first owner had passed away, but his wife was reluctant to sell it, so, for some 12 years it languished in a (luckily dry) garage before the second owner bought it.

After a short while the second owner then sold the car on to the third, in London, and a member of the 1100 Club. David went to view the car and take it for a test drive. He was disappointed, however, to see the owner desperately washing a massive accumulation of leaves off the unloved and faded paintwork. The test drive exposed a very noisy gearbox, which could be heard over the very crackly radio the owner insisted on demonstrating. The issue, as it turned out, was in the intermediate gears, but did not sound very healthy so could have been a big job.

David passed on the car, but, some six weeks later, the owner got back in touch. He was desperate to sell as he was taking up a new job in the USA and had no storage, so David got the car for a very revised offer, and has owned it ever since, with no intention of ever selling it.

After 36 years of ownership the only major jobs David has

Here is David Haycock posing beside his very original 1966 Riley Kestrel.

As David's Riley is a Mark I, it has the extended rear fins that were shortened on the Mark II models.

has never been welded – so is quite a rarity in that respect. The interior is also original, and is nicely mellowed and worn in, while remaining smart and good-looking.

The leather seats, in BMC's colour of Mushroom (a sort of light brown) match the rest of the car's interior panels, and the walnut dash is as fresh as the day it left the factory. All in all the Riley's cockpit is a nice place to be, is very comfortable, and has stood up to the rigours of time very well. The car is, like all ADO16s, surprisingly modern to drive, and David is happy to take the car long distances – if he's not popping up to BMIHT at Gaydon for an 1100 Club event, he's whizzing up to North London for the Enfield Pageant or some other event of interest.

While using the car holds no fear, the only downside is the Riley's motorway performance – as an 1100 it's happy to bop along at 60 to 70 but doesn't have much in reserve at those speeds. David finds the slightly more powerful and higher

carried out have been the repair of the dodgy gearbox and fixing the original but very faded and sorry looking paint. He rebuilt the gearbox himself – it was quite straightforward and only the layshaft needed replacing as its case hardening had failed. The cure for the sorry looking paintwork was a bit more of an effort. It was too far gone to save, so David had the car resprayed in its original colours – two-tone Sandy Beige body and Arianca Beige roof, which nicely matches the original leather and wood trimmed interior. The respray was done some 32 years ago but the paintwork still gleams and the car looks immaculate. The body is also very good, with all original panels and no rust, while the car is still on its original subframes and

The Riley's interior was upmarket compared to the other cars in the range. Its speedometer and tachometer flank a circular instrument cluster with fuel, water temp, and oil pressure gauges.

In the rear, the luxury specification of David Haycock's Riley continues with leather seats.

geared 1300 a better motorway car – as evidenced by his ownership of a few more examples of the ADO16. His stable includes an original Mark I Morris 1100, which he has owned since 1988 and has a mere 16,000 miles on the clock, and he has recently bought a Mark II Austin 1300, which is also very original and well worth preserving.

All in all, David epitomises many ADO16 owners. They are a passionate bunch who really appreciate the innovative engineering and incredible practicality that ADO16 offers. It was sad to see how ADO16 had almost disappeared from the classic scene in the 1990s, and it is only the passion of owners like David who have moved the cars firmly back up and onto the classic map – a position that the cars' original performance, technical innovation and sheer joie de vivre more than justifies.

This view of David Haycock's Riley shows the long fins of the Mark I and how the upper colour of the two-tone paint extended to the top of the boot lid. Note also the 'Riley' badged hubcaps.

David Haycock's Riley engine sports twin SU carburettors. The Riley grille sits in a different front panel to the Austin and Morris cars.

David's little Riley Kestrel is a pleasing-looking car, with a touch of class.

Chapter 4

ADO16 model by model

The top-of-the-range MG version of ADO16 hit the UK market in September 1962, a few months after the Morris version was launched. This is Jim Hills' lovely 1967 example – an MG 1100.

Introduction

This chapter gives a description of each of the main ADO16 models, starting with the 'cooking' models: the Austin and Morris versions; then the sporting numbers, Riley and MG; and the prestige ones, the Wolseley and Vanden Plas models. It also looks at the cars produced abroad, and the unusual variants that appeared in various far flung parts.

The Austin and Morris 'cooking' models

Introduction

ADO16 burst onto the UK market in August 1962 with the announcement of the Morris 1100, quickly followed by the sporting MG 1100 in September of that year. Further models, badged Austin, Riley, Wolseley and Vanden Plas followed. The 1300cc models were introduced in 1967, with all versions gaining the larger engine; otherwise the

The two-door version of the saloon was quite rare in the UK market as most early two-doors were exported. This is the Austin version.

specifications of each 1300 model tended to be the same as the 1100 version.

While production commenced with two- and four-door saloon versions, initially the two-door cars were all destined for export markets, mainly in MG form to the USA, but with Denmark also getting two-door Morris and Austin versions in 1965 to 1967.

Morris 1100 and 1300 – 1962-1973

The first ADO16 models to be introduced were the Morris-badged version and the MG, both introduced in 1962 in 1100 form. The original Morris model came in two body styles, two- or four-door, and both body types were available in Basic or De-luxe trim.

The basic model was reasonably well equipped for the time, although optional extras included the heater, windscreen washer (both standard on the De-luxe model), fresh air equipment, radio, whitewall tyres and laminated windscreen. Export models could also be fitted with a rubber floor mat. The front seats were mounted on runners to allow fore and aft movement, but the seat squab and back were fixed in position. On the three-door models the entire seat tipped forward to allow access to the rear seats.

In De-luxe specification, the exterior was jollied up with an anodised aluminium radiator grille, stainless steel door top trims and waist level finishers replacing the standard car's

The first car in the ADO16 range was the Morris 1100. In this brochure illustration the chrome strip on the bonnet is prominent.

painted items, and two front and two rear chrome overriders on the bumpers.

The interior received a temperature gauge and front door pockets, the pillars and cant rails were plastic coated, and there were two rather than one interior sun visors, plus there was a heater and windscreen washers.

All the cars in the range were fitted with a single stalk mounted on the steering column that controlled the headlamp flasher and dip or main beam, the self cancelling indicators

The Morris 1100 dash had a speedometer opposite the driver, with open cubbyholes on each side.

The interior of ADO16 was surprisingly roomy for its length thanks to the clever packaging of the engine and gearbox. This brochure illustration emphasises the spacious cabin by removing the doors.

and the horn. The only 'safety' feature on the De-luxe was the fitment of two horns, rather than the standard car's single item.

The Morris 1100 and 1300 two- and four-door saloons were no longer sold on the domestic market after the Morris Marina was introduced in 1971, but production did continue for export markets through to 1973.

Austin 1100 and 1300 – 1963-1974

The Austin-badged ADO16 was introduced on the sixth of September, 1963, and came in a single four-door body style and in Basic and De-luxe trims levels, in much the same way as

the Morris 1100. While the bodyshell was identical to the Morris model, the Austin had a new 'wavy' front grille, Austin badges and hubcaps embossed with the Austin 'A'.

While most of the Austin model's interior trim was the same as the Morris variant, the Austin variant was fitted with the strip speedometer, as originally seen on the MG variant, rather than the Morris' binnacle-mounted circular instrument.

Optional extras were limited to a heater, (now called a heater/demister in the brochure), leather seats (or rather leather seat contact surfaces) and a passenger side sun visor for the Basic saloon.

The Austin version of ADO16 came onto the UK market in September 1963. The cars were identical mechanically but had different trimmings.

The estate version was versatile and practical, and was one of the first hatchbacks to appear on the UK market. The whole of the rear door opened, presenting a relatively wide and flat load area. The rear seats could be folded: the backrest could

The Austin and Morris three-door saloon/ estate – 1966-1974

The range gained a new model in 1966 with the introduction of the three-door estate version. This came in two guises: the Morris Traveller and the Austin Countryman, and shared their trim levels with the saloons.

The Austin dashboard sported a strip speedometer as used on the MG variant, but without the wooden trim.

be hinged forward to extend the load bay, and the front of the seat base was hinged so that when it was up it formed a barrier between the load bay and the front seats. Alternatively, the rear seats could be arranged with the upholstery upwards, which, combined with the reclining front seats, formed a bed in the cabin.

The rear side windows were divided into two panes, and could slide open for extra ventilation.

In 1967 after the announcement of the Countryman/Traveller version of ADO16 in 1966, BMC used the three-door design to produce a small number of prototype ADO16 vans. These had metal panels instead of the sliding rear windows and a revised interior to allow for load carrying, but mechanically were identical to the standard passenger cars.

Some 22 were supplied as rolling test beds to Shellmex BP Ltd, the oil distributor, and further examples were supplied to BMC distributors as delivery vans for spare

After the four- and two-door saloons, the third and last version of ADO16 was the estate. Known as the Traveller in Morris form and Countryman when badged as an Austin, this is Roy Robinson's Morris Traveller.

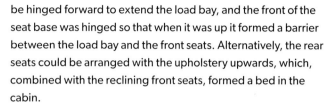

There was a lot of thought put into the estate's seats – the rear seats could be folded down to form a long load bay or reversed to form a double bed with the reclined front seats.

(which would also be applied to the estate versions), but it never materialised, and the van project was quietly dropped.

The Austin 1100 and 1300 range, with two- and four-door saloons to the left and the estate version and 1300GT to the right.

The estate's rear windows were sliding affairs and were locked using the same catches seen on early Minis.

parts, and internally to deliver parts throughout the BMC factory network.

While the van was found to be quiet inside, the interlinked Hydrolastic suspension would raise the nose with consequent loss of traction if a heavy load was carried. Self levelling suspension was considered

Specification tables – Austin and Morris cooking models

Layout   Front engine, transversely mounted. Front-wheel drive. Four-/five-seater, two- or four-door saloon body or three-door hatchback estate of unitary construction. Front and rear rubber mounted subframes to carry all mechanical and suspension components

Engine

Type	Four-cylinder, overhead valve
Block material	Cast iron
Head material	Cast iron
Cylinders	Four in-line
Cooling	Centrifugal pump with water/antifreeze mix
Bore and stroke	1100: 64.59mm x 83.72mm
	1300: 70.61mm x 81.28mm
Capacity	1100: 1098cc
	1300: 1275cc
Valves	Two valves per cylinder, pushrod operated
Compression ratio	1100: 8.5:1
	1300: 8.8:1
Carburettor	1100: Single SU HS2 constant velocity
	1300: Single SU HS4 constant velocity
Max Power 1100	48bhp at 5100rpm
Max Power 1300	60bhp at 5250rpm
Max torque 1100	60ft/lb at 2500rpm
Max torque 1300	69.5ft/lb at 2500rpm
Fuel capacity	8.5 imp galls/38 litres

Transmission

Gearbox (Manual):

Clutch	7⅛in diameter, hydraulically operated	
Ratios	1st	3.63:1
	2nd	2.17:1
	3rd	1.41:1
	4th	1.00:1
Reverse	3.63:1	
Final drive	4.133:1	
Gearbox (Automatic)	Four forward, one reverse, torque converter	

Suspension and steering

Type	Independent all round with interlinked front and rear Hydrolastic displacers
Front	Dual wishbone with unequal levers Swivel axle mounted on ball joints Fore and aft displacement controlled by rubber mounted tie rods
Rear	Trailing arm, with Hydrolastic displacers, auxiliary spring and anti-roll bar
Steering	Rack-and-pinion
Tyres	5.50-12 tubeless
Wheels	Pressed steel with decorative hub caps

Brakes

Type	Girling hydraulic front discs and rear drums
Size (front)	8in (20.32cm) diameter solid discs
Size (Rear)	8in (20.32cm) diameter by 1¼in (3.18cm) width drums
Handbrake	Cable operated from cabin acting on rear drums

Electrical system   12-volt, dynamo (alternator from 1971)

Dimensions

Track	Front: 51½in/130.81cm
	Rear: 50⅞in/129.22cm
Wheelbase	93½in/237.49cm
Overall length	146¾in/372.75cm
Overall width	60⅜in/159.17cm
Overall height	53⅞in/136.84cm
Kerbside weight	1820lb/825.5kg

Approx performance (1100)

Top speed	77mph/124kph
0-60mph	20.2sec

The MG, Riley and 1300GT sports models

Introduction

The MG was the first sport version of the ADO16. and appeared in October 1962 as an 1100cc four-door saloon in the home market and a two- or four-door saloon in export (mainly US) markets.

Jim Hills' 1967 MG 1100 is a rare survivor. Note the MG grille and the two-tone paintwork that extends down to the car's waistline and bonnet top, unlike the two-tone finish on the Riley.

The sporting MG was joined in the range by the Riley version in September 1965, but, unlike the MG, was available only in four-door form. The Riley did have a slightly more luxurious interior than the MG.

The final sporty number was the Austin and Morris 1300GT, which effectively replaced the Riley in 1969 and gained some very 1970s paint schemes in 1971 when its Mark III incarnation arrived. All the sports models offered twin-carburettors and a small power boost over the standard cars.

The Riley's two-tone paintwork only goes down to the window line, unlike the MG. This is David Haycock's car; another rare survivor in very original condition.

In profile, the four-door saloon does not give the sporting impression expected of an MG, with only the two-tone paint and MG badges on the hubcaps giving the game away. Note the Mark I's long rear fins.

The MG 1100 and 1300 – 1962-1973

The 'pocket rocket' MG 1100 was introduced in October 1962, and was initially only available in four-door specification on the home market, although the US market was given the two-door model. UK customers would have to wait until the introduction of the Mark II model in 1967 before they could buy a two-door MG 1100, but they did get the option of a 1300cc engine in the summer of 1967.

The Mark II MG model was introduced in October 1967, and was available in 1100 and 1300 guises, but only in two-door format to avoid competition with the Riley Kestrel, and in 1969 the 1100 version was dropped. The MG 1300 Mark II continued in production through to 1973, some two years after the Mark III was introduced – but it is unclear if the MG was ever given the Mark III label. The MG was withdrawn from the home market during 1971, but continued in production for export markets until 1973.

Based on the original 1100, the MG version had a new front

BMC World's Largest Producers of Front — Wheel — Powered Vehicles. Over a Million sold

The MG was available in a single colour or two-tone paint, as shown by this original brochure picture. Two- or four-door versions were available but not many two-doors made it onto the UK market.

The interior was very similar to the Austin variant, with a strip speedometer flanked by a fuel and temperature gauge, central ash tray and glovebox opposite the passenger. The main change was the use of wood trim on the dash rather than the original's brushed metal finish. The door cards were trimmed in two colours.

end, with a neat MG chromed grille and new circular combined side and indicator lights. Other external changes were slim chrome waist trims running the length of the car at waist height and across the boot lid, an octagonal 'MG' badge on the right-hand side of the boot lid, and the option of two-tone paintwork. The division between the two colours was the waist line trim strip, the bonnet line, and the centre horizontal line of the boot lid.

Mechanically, the main change was the uprated engine with twin SU carburettors that pushed out a heady 55bhp.

In 1968, the year after the Mark II was introduced, the more sporting three-dial (speedometer, rev counter and ancillary instruments) dashboard was introduced, along with a new smaller and sportier steering wheel, and new switchgear was introduced.

The Riley Kestrel – 1965-1969

THE Riley Kestrel was produced only in four-door form throughout its life. The Riley Kestrel 1100 Mark I was produced from September 1965, and was then replaced with the 1100 Mark II version from October 1967. In October 1968 the Riley was given the 1300 engine unit and the car was simply named the Riley 1300. At this point the car was also given the option of being fitted with the AP automatic gearbox. The Riley 1300 ceased production in July 1969, when the model was replaced by the Mark II 1300GT.

Based on the original four-door 1100, the Mark I Kestrel had a redesigned front end that incorporated a traditional Riley-styled chromed radiator grille flanked by low level chromed grilles that carried the side lights and indicators. Two-tone paint was an option, with the dividing line being the lower window line, so only the top of the bonnet, the pillars and the roof would be in the top colour.

To avoid competing directly with the sporty MG variant, the Riley had a higher level of interior trim, blending a little luxury with the sporting appeal. Leather seats and a walnut dashboard gave the interior the required ambiance, while a full set of three circular instruments, comprising speedo, rev counter and a

The Riley was aimed at the customer with an active lifestyle who wanted a bit of luxury with their sporting saloon. This brochure picture sums it all up nicely.

As with the MG, from the profile, it is only the Riley's two-tone paint and badged hubcaps that say this is not a cooking Austin or Morris.

combined cluster faced the driver. The combined instrument cluster gave fuel, temperature and oil pressure gauges. The standard steering wheel featured a Riley horn press, and the hub caps featured Riley badges. With a 55bhp twin-carburettor power plant the car was identical mechanically to the MG.

The Austin and Morris 1300GT – 1969-1974

The GT version of the Austin and Morris 1300 was introduced in 1969. It replaced the Riley version in the range, and was sold alongside the sporty MG model, which continued to be produced. With the 1300GT, British Leyland produced a creditable GT car by utilising the MG's twin-carb engine, slightly lowering the suspension from the standard cars, and revamping the interior to give a sporting three-dial dash, including a rev counter, and dressing up the outside in a new range of colours and trim.

The most striking feature of the exterior was a black vinyl roof, along with a matt black radiator grille that featured a red 'GT' badge and a pair of chrome horizontal trim strips. Special wheel trims with nine chrome 'spokes' on a matt black background were fitted, along with a wide chrome and black rubber trim strip along the waistline, and a 'GT' badge on each 'C' pillar. Colours were Glacier White, Flame Red or Bronze Yellow, while the interiors were all black.

The only difference between the Austin or Morris versions was the name on the top of the new front grille.

The last of the sporting ADO16s was the 1300GT – which was badged as either Austin or Morris. In this case, it's an Austin.

Inside the cars had a sporting three-spoke steering wheel with five drilled holes on each spoke, a black vinyl covered dashboard with eyeball vents at each end, a central ashtray, and a glovebox with lid opposite the passenger. The driver had a matching circular speedometer and rev counter, and a third circular instrument cluster for the fuel and temperature gauges. A pair of rocker switches on the right-hand side operated the lights and wipers.

While the headlining was white plastic with black printed dots to make it look as if it was perforated, the rear quarter panels, carpets, sun visors and door cars were black.

The 1300GT had a sporty interior, with the all-black dash with a large circular speedometer and tachometer, plus a third circular gauge cluster giving fuel, water temperature and oil pressure. This is John Norris' example.

Mechanically the car was pretty much identical to the MG version, and, like the rest of the range, the dynamo was replaced with an alternator in 1972, and the electrics changed to negative earth.

The main distinguishing feature of the Mark III 1300GT was its selection of flamboyant exterior colours, a heady mixture of what are seen now as classic 1970s colours comprising: Aqua, Green Mallard, Limeflower, Black Tulip and Harvest Gold,

Under the bonnet, the 1300GT had twin-carburettors and a brake servo.

which were complemented with a choice of Olive or Navy Blue interiors.

Specification tables for the sports models

Layout   Front engine, transversely mounted. Front-wheel drive. Four-/five seater two- or four-door saloon body or three-door hatchback estate of unitary construction. Front and rear rubber mounted subframes to carry all mechanical and suspension components.

Engine

Type   Four-cylinder, overhead valve

Block material	Cast iron
Head material	Cast iron
Cylinders	Four in-line
Cooling	Centrifugal pump with water/antifreeze mix
Bore and stroke	1100: 64.59mm x 83.72mm
	1300: 70.61mm x 81.28mm
Capacity	1100: 1098cc
	1300: 1275cc
Valves	Two valves per cylinder, pushrod operated
Compression ratio	1100: 8.9:1 (optional 8.1:1)
	1300: 8.8:1
Carburettor	1100: Twin SU HS2 constant velocity
	1300: Single SU HS4 constant velocity
Max Power 1100	55bhp at 5500rpm
Max Power 1300GT	70bhp at 6000rpm
Max torque 1100	61ft/lb at 2750rpm
Max torque 1300GT	74ft/lb at 3250rpm
Fuel capacity	8.5 Imp Galls/38 litres

Transmission

Gearbox (Manual):		
Clutch	7⅛in (diameter, hydraulically operated	
Ratios	1st	3.63:1
	2nd	2.17:1
	3rd	1.41:1
	4th	1.00:1

Reverse	3.63:1
Final drive	4.133:1
Gearbox (Automatic)	Four forward, one reverse, torque converter.

Suspension and steering

Type	Independent all round with interlinked front and rear Hydrolastic displacers
Front	Dual wishbone with unequal levers. Swivel axle mounted on ball joints. Fore and aft displacement controlled by rubber mounted tie rods.
Rear	Trailing arm, with Hydrolastic displacers, auxiliary spring and anti-roll bar
Steering	Rack-and-pinion
Tyres	5.50-12 tubeless
Wheels	Pressed steel with decorative hub caps

Brakes

Type	Girling hydraulic front discs and rear drums
Size (front) MG1100	8in (20.32cm) diameter solid discs
Size (front) 1300GT	8.39in (21cm) diameter solid discs
Size (Rear)	8in (20.32cm) diameter by 1¼in (3.18cm) width drums
Handbrake	Cable operated from cabin acting on rear drums

Electrical system | 12-volt, dynamo (alternator from 1971)

Dimensions

Track	Front: 51½in/130.81cm
	Rear: 50⅞in/129.22cm
Wheelbase	93½in/237.49cm
Overall length	146¾inches/372.75cm
Overall width	60⅜in/159.17cm
Overall height	53⅞in/136.84cm
Kerbside weight	MG 1100: 1852lb/840kg

Approx performance (MG 1100)

Top speed	82mph/132kph
0–60mph	16.5 sec

Jim Hills stands by his very original MG 1100.

Jim Hills' 1967 MG 1100 Mark I

Jim Hills' experience with ADO16s goes back a long way. When he was still at school in the 1960s his Saturday job was to de-wax and prepare factory fresh cars at his granddad's car dealership in Blackwater, Surrey, which – and you guessed it – was a BMC franchise. He spent many happy hours (well not so happy – it was a messy and hard job) getting all the factory protective coatings and wax off the paintwork, along with the sticky brown paper and the resulting residue used to protect the chrome in transit. He worked on a fair few ADO16s along the way, and this helped to instil an affection for the car that has lasted to this day.

Another ADO16 tale from his dealership days includes mention of the propensity for the cars to rust – he found it not uncommon to have an ADO16 fail its first MOT test at three years old, thanks to rust. One of the more amusing tales was when a chap brought in a five- or six-year old MG 1100 as a part exchange. Jim's grandfather had his own way of testing ADO16s for rust. It was simple; jack up the rear of the car, and if the body went up and the wheels remained on the floor then he refused the part-exchange ... The MG owner watched this occur, then, having had the body dropped back onto the errant rear subframe, drove off, never to be seen again.

All this insider knowledge stood Jim in good stead when he and his mates started to drive. Obviously, being young lads with a need for speed, they wanted to start their driving careers

Above: The rear quarter of Jim Hills' 1967 MG 1100 shows its original two-tone paintwork and the long fins of a Mark I car.

Top, right: This is where Jim Hills' love of MG 1100s started – this is him back in 1971 with his original MG 1100 outside his house.

Right: And here he is a couple of years ago in the same spot with his current MG 1100 – while it's not the same car, it is to the same specification.

in something sporty, but the UK insurance companies were wise to this, and the cost of insurance for anything remotely sporty was prohibitive, even back in 1971. Except, that is, for the MG 1100, which was, insurance wise, very reasonable and

From the front, the MG's dominating feature is the traditional chrome grille, which gives the car a completely different look from the cooking models.

affordable. So Jim and three or four of his mates were soon tooling around in nippy little MG 1100s, as the sporty little saloons had slipped under the underwriters' radar.

These experiences made a deep impression on Jim and

led him to buy his current 1967 MG 1100. It is to exactly the same specification as his first car – one that he regrets not really looking after whilst an impetuous youth, and which has long since gone to the great scrapyard in the sky. The accompanying photos show Jim – in one a young, long-haired slim youth standing by his pride and joy outside his then house; the second, a greyer-haired, slightly larger and more mature gentleman standing by his new pride and joy outside the same house some 45 years later. He did interrupt the current owners' Sunday lunch when he went to ask permission to take the new photograph, but they didn't seem to mind too much ...

When Jim decided to get another MG 1100 his ambition was to find an original car that hadn't been restored. It took him a couple of years to find his car but what he finally bought is brilliant. With Smoke Grey over Old English White two-tone paintwork, and rather fetching Reef Blue seats and trim, his example is pretty much original and untouched – there's no evidence of welding, the mechanical parts are all original, all the chrome work is present and correct, and it's probably as close to factory fresh as is possible. It even smells right: while it's lost the new car smell, Jim's MG has just the right aroma of 1960s car plastics, slightly musty old carpets, some random hydrocarbons from the twin SU carbs, and a touch of oil to let you know you are in a lovingly maintained classic from the 1960s.

At over half a century old, though, what's the car like

RIght: The rear three-quarter view of Jim Hills' MG 1100 shows off its two-tone paintwork to good effect ...

Below: ... and ornate rear boot latch and numberplate plinth.

to drive? Driving to the photo location, the MG still rides beautifully, the Hydrolastic system still working away to give a soft, compliant and roll free ride, which was surprisingly good for its age. There were no creaks, thuds or rattles thanks to the obvious integrity of the rust-free bodyshell and well looked after mechanicals, and the car displays a surprisingly sprightly performance – its get up and go belying the 55bhp of the A-series – and the induction roar (well, burble) from the twin SUs added to the performance feel.

What's the best thing about the car? Jim loves its unmolested state, its factory paint (you can see on the roof where years of polishing have worn it away in places), the overall patina of the car that says 'I've seen a bit of life and have had a little wear and tear but I'm still just as good as ever.'

The worst thing about the car? Jim thinks it's the gearbox. The lack of synchromesh on first gear can sometimes be a pain. Also, while four speeds were de-rigour at the time, today's drivers would expect five speeds, if only for more relaxed motorway driving. Finally, the brakes also feel a bit 'dead' but he hopes a new set of pads will increase the feel. Otherwise,

Jim is made up with the little MG – not only does it bring back all sorts of memories for him, it also links him back to his youth when he and his mates thrashed around the lanes of North Hampshire in their little posse of sporty MG 1100s. Today, Jim simply loves his little MG, and it gives him a buzz every time he drives it – which is the main thing!

The prestige ones – Wolseley and Vanden Plas

Introduction

There were two 'prestige' versions of the 1100 range: the Wolseley and the Vanden Plas. While the Wolseley versions were made 'on the line' alongside the other MG, 1300GT and Riley variants, the Vanden Plas models were then trimmed and finished off at the Vanden Plas works in London.

The Wolseley 1100 and 1300 – 1965-1973

The Wolseley 1100 was introduced in September 1965, the same time as as the Riley variant, and was available only as a

Top, right: The Wolseley version of ADO16 was probably equivalent to the Riley, but slightly less sporty and with a luxury interior. Obviously sailing was the pastime for Wolseley and Riley customers, as this brochure cover shows.
Right: The Wolseley interior was plush and comfortable. While it was not up to Vanden Plas standards, it was a cut above the Austin and Morris variants.

This is a Wolseley 1300 Mark II. The front grille and sidelight treatment were unique to the model, as was the 45-degree back sweep of the front wing chrome trim strip.

On two-tone cars the front of the car up to the 45-degree strip, the top of the bonnet up to the windscreen, and the sides of the car above the waist trim and below the window line were painted in one colour, and the rest of the car in the other colour.

The Wolseley variant was very similar in mechanical and interior specification to the Riley, with the same 55bhp engine and running gear but retaining the Austin style strip speedometer, fuel and temperature gauges and a polished walnut faced dashboard.

Vanden Plas Princess

The Vanden Plas Mark I was introduced at the London Motor show in October 1963, and was placed into production in early 1964. Initially the car was fitted with the 55bhp twin-carb 1100 engine unit, but a few cars received the 1300cc unit in the

four-door with manual gearbox. In October 1967 the Mark II 1100 version was introduced, and came with the option of the AP automatic gearbox. The 1300cc engine was introduced in 1968. The Wolseley Mark III replaced the Mark II in September 1971 and continued in production until April 1973.

As with the Riley, the main change from the standard model was a revised front end, featuring a chrome Wolseley radiator grille flanked by a pair of chrome trimmed lower grilles, which, in turn, had a pair of horizontal flutes and housed the standard car's combined side and indicator lights. The main difference (apart from the grille) was the use of swept back chrome trim on the front wing, which swept down from the front of the waist trim to the wheelarch at about 45 degrees.

Sitting at the top of the ADO16 tree was the Vanden Plas Princess. The largest grille in the range and a pair of spotlights set off the front end, while pinstripes defined the sides, and 'P' for 'Princess' badges graced the hubcaps.

the boot lid carried 'Vanden Plas' and Princess '1100' italic script badges on each side of the numberplate. Also at the rear was a unique bumper that wrapped around the rear to the wheelarch, and was fitted with larger overriders than the standard car. A built in reversing lamp was incorporated in the rear numberplate light plinth on the rear bumper.

The wheels were painted black, and had chrome rings fitted to the outside of the rims, and the chrome hub caps had central 'VP' badges.

While the exterior of the car was restrained and quite tasteful, it was the inside of the car that received the real luxury treatment, being exquisitely trimmed and built.

summer of 1967. The Mark II was introduced in October 1967 in 1100 form, and this was replaced in 1968 with the 1300cc version.

The car received the same exterior treatment as its MG, Riley and Wolseley brothers, with a prominent 'classic' styled grille on the front complemented by a pair of recessed fog or running lights on each side and a wraparound side and tail light fitting.

A hand painted coach line was applied down each flank, and

The Princess' interior was hand-built and fitted at Vanden Plas in London. Leather seats, walnut veneer door cappings and, of course, a walnut dash made the front seats very special. Rear seat passengers in the Princess were not forgotten. The rear doors got their own walnut capping, leather seats were fitted of course, and walnut veneer picnic tables were fitted onto the backs of the front seats so the rear seat passengers could eat in luxury.

Starting with the roof, its lining was made from 'West of England' cloth. The door caps were trimmed with polished walnut, which matched the polished walnut dashboard.

The dashboard housed a pair of circular recessed instruments opposite the driver – a speedometer and an instrument cluster with fuel and temperature gauges – and to the right of these was a square recessed switch panel. In the centre of the dash was the ashtray, above which was an analogue clock (this could be labelled either Smiths or Jaeger) and opposite the passenger was a lidded glovebox.

At each end of the dash there was a small, circular, adjustable fresh air nozzle, and mounted on the lower edge of the dash were the heater controls.

The seat surfaces were trimmed in Connelly leather, and the reclining fronts were fitted with individual central armrests, while the rears shared a single central armrest. There were fold-up picnic tables, faced with polished walnut veneer, incorporated into the front seat backs. Wilton carpets covered the floor, and even the boot floor was carpeted.

While the Vanden Plas was standard mechanically, all the extra luxury fitment meant the car's weight had crept up – the 1100 version weighed in at 1950lb, which, when compared to the Morris 1100's 1820lb, was the reason for the Vanden Plas' blunted performance – the luxury car's 0-60 time was around a lethargic 21 seconds. All in all though, the Vanden Plas' interior was built to the best British 'Luxury Car' standards, and made it really rather special.

The 'foreign' cars

Introduction

ADO16 was a truly international project, with British-built cars being exported all around the world, and assembled, with varying levels of local content, at a number of assembly plants. The overseas plants were either BMC-owned or co-owned with local producers, and ADO16s were assembled in Spain, Australia, New Zealand and South Africa. Kits of parts, described as Completely Knocked Down (CKD), were exported from the UK factories and assembled in the foreign plants, again with varying levels of local parts added. Local content was usually based on a particular country's legislation at the time. Usually the local content would be the bodyshell, although, in some markets, such as Australia and South Africa, complex mechanical parts, such as engines and gearboxes, would also be locally produced.

New Zealand

In February 1963 the first Austin 1100 produced in New Zealand rolled off Associated Motor Industries' assembly line in its Petone Plant, near Wellington on the south end of North Island. Morris 1100s were assembled by Dominion Motors based at Newmarket, in Auckland, at the north end of North Island, with the first Morris-badged cars appearing in late 1964.

All the cars were assembled from kits of parts supplied from the UK, and were mainly built to UK specification. The plants also assembled MG, Riley and Wolseley variants.

Associated Motor Industries and Dominion Motors merged to form the New Zealand Motor Vehicles in 1969, and the final ADO16s to be assembled were completed in 1976.

The USA

The first model shipped to the US from 1962 was the two-door MG 1100, which was called the 'MG Sports Sedan'. This was a standard MG 1100 but in left-hand drive form, and was sold in the US until the end of the Mark I range in late 1967.Between 1964 and 1966 the US market also received the MG Princess. This was essentially a Vanden Plas 1100 four-door saloon with MG badges. The thinking behind this exercise was to offer a more luxurious MG Sedan, and the car met the brief, but few were actually sold.

The MG Sports Sedan was replaced from early 1968 with the Austin America. These were, as the name suggests primarily aimed at the US market, but some made their way to Canada and Switzerland, thanks to those countries' strict emissions laws.

The America was based on the two-door shell and, in order to meet the emissions legislation in the USA, the cars were fitted with a modified engine complete with emissions control equipment and had the fuel tank modified to stop fuel vapour from escaping to the outside world.

Powered by a single SU carburretored-engine with an 8.8:1 compression ratio giving 58bhp at 5250rpm and 69ft/lb of torque at 3000rpm. The cars were available with either manual or AP automatic gearboxes.

The cars had additional safety equipment, including dual circuit brakes and a laminated windscreen. Inside the car the safety theme continued with the fitment of a brake pressure warning light with test function, front seat catches to prevent the seats tipping forward (later cars had sliding front seats with

From 1968, ADO16 was sold in the USA as the Austin America. The America was fitted with emissions compliant equipment and was based on the two-door saloon.

tipping backs to give access to the rear seats), three-point seat belts in the front and rear seat lap belts, positive-lock door latches and front seat headrests.

Externally there were obvious giveaways to the revised specification, with side marker lights and reflectors fitted to the front and rear wings. The heater was standard, except for cars destined for Hawaii and Puerto Rico.

Finally, the cars were fitted with hazard warning lights and had rubber-coated overriders that met the US collision regulations mandating minimal damage in the event of a minor shunt. Colour were Damask Red, Sable, Pale Primrose, British Racing Green, Riviera Blue and Snowberry While.

The Australians

Introduced in February 1964, the first Australian-built ADO16s were all four-door saloon versions. These Australian versions of the ADO16 had much more local content than most other foreign models, thanks to the Nuffield (ie Morris) investment in its Australian subsidiary. This meant that the Australians could produce virtually everything needed, including engines, gearboxes, and bodyshells, to build the cars. The Australians also had the engineering and design expertise, along with their local experience, to modify the UK designs to meet the different environment in which their home-produced vehicles had to perform.

In the case of the ADO16, this meant that, to cater for the many unmade roads, the cars had extensive additional dustproofing, and stone shields were fitted under the car to protect the engine and fuel tank. The interior gained a front bench seat to allow for three abreast seating. To accommodate the central passenger, there was a new long 'wand'-type gearlever (similar to that fitted to the first Minis), and the handbrake lever was repositioned by the driver's door. A steel 'Venetian' blind for the rear window and an external front sun visor could be specified, and the interior carpets were replaced with more practical rubber mats. The 1100 engine used in the initial models was badged as 'Fireflash'.

During 1966, the Australians introduced a five-door hatchback version, called the YD09 and marketed as the Morris Nomad. The 1300-engined variant of these models was called the Morris 1100S and was fitted with the AP automatic gearbox. In June 1969, the range was revamped with a new range, coded YDO15. This was broadly similar to the Mark II ADO16 with four doors but with two engine options – a 1275cc powered Morris 1300S, similar in specification to the previous Morris 1100S, and the Morris 1500, which was powered by a 1500cc overhead camshaft E series engine, as used in the forthcoming Maxi. The Morris 1300S came with the four-speed automatic gearbox. The 1500 unit initially had a four-speed manual gearbox, but from 1971 a five-speed box was available. YDO15 also benefited from larger 6.20 x 12 wheels and tyres. The Morris Nomad five-door lived on in 1300 and 1500 engine guise. However, sales of the revamped models were not good, and production ended in 1971.

Italian Innocenti

Innocenti was an engineering company based in Milan. In 1959, it had signed an agreement with BMC to assemble various BMC models, including the Austin A40. Part of the agreement gave Innocenti the right to modify the BMC products for the Italian market. With ADO16, Innocenti made a number of changes to the cars. In April 1963, it was announced that Innocenti would produce its version of ADO16 as the Innocenti IM3, and by May, assembly had started at the Milan plant.

Changes from the standard UK model were numerous, including an all-Italian wiring system with additional fuses, relay-operated headlamps and horns, engine bay and boot lights, as well as reversing lights incorporated into a new numberplate light plinth. The dash was modified to carry a pair of round instrument clusters, and the steering wheel angle was altered with the incorporation of a pair of universal joints in the steering column. An easy recognition feature was the fitment of a flush flap covering the fuel filler cap. The car was fitted from the word go with the MG specification twin-carburettor engine and was fitted with a brake servo and new hubcaps on new steel wheels.

The IM3 was replaced by the IM3S with some minor updates, such as deleting the bumper overriders. Some cars substituted Dell'Orto carbs for the SU units. The model was then replaced in 1964 by the I4. This model was powered by the single-carburettor engine and was supplemented by the I4S powered by the MG unit. Apart from minor differences in external trim, the I4 and I4S were very much a revamp of the existing UK Mark I models with an Italian interior. The I5 was introduced in late 1970 and still used the Mark I bodyshell with its long rear wings. It was powered by the twin-carb engine. Sales were slow, and the model was dropped in September 1974.

Chile

ADO16 production in Chile was undertaken by a British Leyland-owned subsidiary company, British Leyland Automotores de Chile SA. This was based in Arica, right up in the north of Chile on the Pacific coast. However, the site was some 1500 miles north of the main Chilean steel industry, which was based in Concepción. So the decision was made to construct the bodyshell of a two-door MG version of ADO16 out of fibreglass, with steel tubing reinforcement. This would also meet the country's requirement for at least 55% local input, and the engines and other mechanical elements were shipped in from the UK. Production eventually started in 1971 and then ceased in 1974.

South Africa

Exports of ADO16 to South Africa started in 1962, and by

1963 ADO16s were being assembled in CKD form by the BMC plant sited in Blackheath in Cape Province. Initially, the plant assembled Austin and MG saloons. Then, Wolseley 1100s were added to the mix during 1966, initially in twin-carb form but then detuned in 1967 to only one carburettor. Estate versions badged Austin and Morris appeared in May 1967.

Two new models were introduced in 1968 in the form of the Austin 11/55 and the Wolseley 11/55, both powered by a development of the single-carb A-series 1100 unit, which gave 55bhp thanks to larger inlet valves, a bigger carburettor, and a modified air filter.

The most radical change using ADO16 as a basis was a Giovanni Michelotti designed 'three-box' revision to the original design, which was created for British Leyland but never produced for the UK market. The new three-box car, when built in South Africa, was named the Austin Apache. This resulted in a more traditionally shaped small saloon that, while it kept the ADO16 centre section, sported a longer (and larger) boot and a completely restyled front end, with a very Triumph 2000 look with a pair of small headlamps at either end of a flat front radiator grille. These changes increased the front and rear overhangs and made the overall car some 13 inches (33 cm) longer overall.

The design was also adopted by the Spanish and produced in Spain in the form of the Authi Victoria. Three Apache models were sold in South Africa, and the original version was introduced in 1971. This was powered by the 1275cc single-carb A-series engine and featured a new through-flow ventilation system. A twin-carb version followed in TC form, offering improved performance thanks to its 75bhp engine and featuring a rev counter and sports steering wheel and vinyl roof. The final variant was a limited edition of 300 'luxury' cars, called the Apache 3S Special, which had brown brushed nylon upholstery and deep pile carpet. All were painted in Harvest Gold with a light brown vinyl roof and Rostyle type steel wheels and automatic gearboxes. Production of the Apache continued into 1978.

Spain

Set up in 1965 with a new assembly plant in Pamplona, close to the French border in Navarra, Spain, Authi was a joint venture company formed between BMC and a Spanish company. It produced CKD cars in order to avoid the Spanish government's excessive taxes charged on foreign manufactured cars.

Originally, the company produced left-hand drive versions of the standard MG 1100 from 1967, quickly followed by an Austin 1300 derivative. However, there was a desire for the factory to have its own product and more local content, so the company started to produce its own version of Michelotti's three-box design to update its range.

In Spain, the new car was known as the Authi Victoria and went into production in 1972. There were two versions,

The Spanish Austin Victoria was an ADO16 with a new front and rear end, styled by Giovanni Michelotti. It was also produced in South Africa and had the looks of the Mark II Triumph 2000.

Victoria but, in 1974, a catastrophic fire at Pamplona destroyed the plant and associated stocks of spares and parts destined for production. With British Leyland in trouble, Authi did not survive, and the plant was sold off to Seat in 1976.

Owners' impressions
John Norris' Austin 1300GT

At the time of writing, John Norris is the 1100 Club's area representative for Hampshire, and owns a Teal Blue Austin 1300 GT. This is not his first ADO16; he has been immersed in the cars from a very early age. His first car was a Morris Minor Traveller, and this was the car that he used after passing his test (first time after only three lessons) at the tender age of 17, in 1990. A few months later, John's father, who managed a large, well-known British Leyland dealership, Wadham Stringer of Gosport, suggested he buy a Morris 1100 which had come in as part exchange for a new Metro, registration number THO 803H.

The car was a one-owner-from-new car and was a bit of a bargain at £50. After a touch of TLC, it introduced John to the sophistication of the ADO16 when compared to the 'previous generation' Minor. He was impressed by the braking, with the 1100's front discs far outperforming the Minor's drums.

both powered by the 1300 unit, and comprised the standard Victoria, with single oblong headlamps, and the De-luxe, with a 68bhp engine and quadruple round headlights, two at each end of the grille. The pair of Victorias were joined in 1974 by a version of the Mark III ADO16 two-box saloon.

The company was developing a Mark II version of the

John Norris' Morris 1300GT is a fine example of the last model of ADO16 produced, and has won a number of 1100 Club awards. Its peppy performance places it firmly at the performance end of the model range.

A black grille and GT badging set the exterior apart from the other Mark III models. John Norris' example wears a set of period alloy wheels.

The 1100's Hydrolastic suspension gave a much better ride than the Minor's, and the all-around independent suspension gave the 1100 far superior handling as well. The car benefited from numerous improvements. Over the Christmas period of 1991, the engine was overhauled in two days – getting a new crankshaft and bearings, oil pump, clutch, and timing chain.

Then in early 1992, an errant driver drove into the 1100, damaging the rear wing, which was repaired under insurance. On 16th August 1992, THO 803H was chosen to attend the 1100 Club's 30th Anniversary ADO16 rally at the Longbridge works, and, so it was looking its best, John fitted two new front wings and four new doors, with the respray being done by the same body shop that had repaired the rear wing previously.

The 1100 served as John's daily driver for a couple of years, and so besotted with ADO16s was he, and thirsting for a bit more performance, that the next car to join his fleet in 1993 was a Flame Red 1972 Austin 1300GT. By then John and his dad were both enthusiastic members of the 1100 Club, and the car had turned up in the 1100 Club's magazine *Idle Chatter*. The extra performance and sportier nature were appreciated, and the 1300GT rapidly displaced the 1100 as John's daily driver.

Of course, two ADO16s just weren't enough, and in 1995 John was approached to see if he wanted an Austin 1300 Estate. The car was in a bit of a state, with a slipping clutch and smoky engine, so John walked away but relented a couple of weeks later and bought the car for its scrap value – a mere £25. As well

as the mechanical woes the car's body was a bit tatty, with bad paint and dodgy sills, so, after repairs, John resprayed the car himself.

The estate was put to work on club duties, and was especially convenient for transporting the Hampshire area's club paraphernalia around the country! However, times changed, and eventually, in 2004, John's parents moved to Wales, the cars were sold, and the family left the club.

The ADO16 itch is a hard one to scratch, and by 2015, John had rejoined the 1100 Club with the intention of finding another ADO16 – specifically, a 1300GT. In November 2018, he was back in the fold with his current car: a 1972 Teal Blue Austin 1300GT. The car has had only three owners – the original owner kept it from 1972 to 2016, when it was passed to the second owner who only kept it for a couple of years before John bought it in November 2018. And the car is everything John remembered from his other examples – it is nippy, keeps up with modern traffic, and gives good miles per gallon. The only downside, as far as John is concerned, is the interior – he is not too keen on Limeflower, but he's coming round to it and recognizes it is very much 'of its time.'

Although it had only a few owners, the car was not perfect, and John has done a fair amount of work to bring it up to its current super condition. This has included general servicing, a new carpet set, a new high-performance 'Maniflow' exhaust, an inlet manifold kit to give some extra oomph and, finally, the biggest

From the rear quarter, John Norris' 1300GT shows the clean lines shared with the rest of the range, and its Teal Blue paintwork.

An example of John Norris' ceramic ADO16 – in this case, a replica of his own 1300GT.

job, a respray. The painting was done at home by John using cellulose Teal Blue paint and a cheap compressor. Completed on the hottest day of July 2019, the respray stands up to the closest scrutiny and is a credit to John's skills. The icing on the cake was the fitment of genuine period 'British Leyland' mud flaps.

As well as the performance manifold, modifications include electronic ignition, a sport coil, Accuspark 'Triple Strike' spark plugs, a security tracker, and genuine period Dunlop D1 Alloy wheels and new tires. All this work has paid off with the car winning a number of prizes including Best GT at the 50th-anniversary meet at Milton Keynes in 2019, a Highly Commended at the August 2022 60th Anniversary 1100 Club National Meet at Cogges Manor Farm, Oxfordshire, and gained a Highly Commended at the September 2022 60th Anniversary Meeting at Milton Keynes.

All the way back in 1993, John's family set up a pottery business and commissioned a large pottery money box design based on the 1100.

The models are 11.5 inches long, 5 inches wide, and 4.5 inches high, and are available in various colour and trim combinations, including, of course, a Teal Blue 1300GT version. Now thirty years later, John still produces a few models each year, which are available for sale at events up and down the country. Look out for a Teal Blue 1300 GT at a show, and you are sure to see these great models on display!

As the Hampshire area representative for the 1100 Club, John is looking forward to many more years attending events, showing his GT, and, of course, driving the car for pleasure.

Chapter 5

Owning and running

Now a rare sight on UK roads, the estate version of ADO16 was a versatile and useful little car. This is Roy Robinson's fine example.

Introduction

Owning and running a member of the ADO16 family can be a rewarding experience, and the cars are generally reliable while offering an adequate level of performance in today's traffic, and a surprising degree of comfort thanks to the Hydrolastic suspension. The cars do need regular maintenance, and service intervals are short compared to modern cars. However, maintenance largely involves ensuring the oil and filter are replaced regularly, and items such as plugs and points are cleaned and adjusted. Thanks to the light weight and relatively low performance of the cars, the brake pads and shoes last a

long time. Still, the front disc calipers can seize if the car is not used for a while, and the rear slave cylinder seals can fail due to corrosion if the brake fluid is not renewed regularly. The Hydrolastic suspension is reliable and long-lived, but if fluid has leaked out, the suspension will sag – usually on one side, requiring a special pump to recharge the units. While these pumps are not widely available, many classic mechanics will have them on hand. In general, the ADO16 is a low-maintenance car, with most jobs being easy to do and well within the reach of reasonably competent owners.

Bodywork

The condition of the bodywork of any ADO16 is critical, and the original design did have a number of rust traps and rust-prone areas. The rear of the front wings is particularly prone to rust as road dirt can accumulate in the crevasse behind the wheel. Leaving wet, caked-on mud there is a recipe for disaster. The result will be paint bubbles just ahead of the door shut line. If these are present, then the wing will need replacement or repair, and it is likely that the front inner wings will also need repair.

The underside of the car is also prone to rusting, particularly around the rear subframe mounts. These are difficult to repair and will need the subframe to be dropped – a big job. The rear subframe itself is also vulnerable and, again, is tricky to repair. Luckily, as the A-series engine can exhibit a certain amount of 'incontinence,' the front subframe and its mounts, along with a fair proportion of the front end, are usually quite well-protected from corrosion by the film of oil deposited from the engine! Wheelarches are usually not too bad, but an accumulation of road muck on their inside edges will eventually lead to them rotting out.

While the cars are built from good-quality steel, their various rust traps and general age make them vulnerable to rust. In general, it is well worth investing in one of the proprietary rust-proofing waxes or oils and getting them inside the various box sections, including the sills, and keeping the treatment topped up every year or so. Also, make sure that any rust traps are kept clear of any clinging mud and that the paint protecting the metal in any trap is in good condition. With these few precautions, the cars can be protected from rust and will last a long time with a little care.

Mechanical upgrades

Introduction

Surprisingly for such an old design, there are not very many mechanical upgrades or modifications that a keen owner can add that actually improve the car. ADO16's mechanical underpinnings were well thought out and understood when the car was introduced thanks to the manufacturer's experience in producing the Mini, so the cars were pretty reliable from the word go.

Electronic ignition

The question of fitting electronic ignition is always contentious. There is a school of thought that the standard points system is reliable, does not go out of adjustment too quickly, and, in the event of a failure, can be fixed by anyone with a bit of mechanical know-how.

ADO16 was first produced as a four-door saloon car, and the four-door was the most popular in terms of sales over the model's life. This is Dean Oakey's 1300 Mark II.

There are two readily available electronic ignition systems, however. The first simply replaces the points and condenser with an electronic switch (usually triggered by magnets) that fits inside the existing distributor and uses the existing advance-retard unit. The second is a full-blown electronic system, which usually has a switch unit in the distributor and an external control box to control advance and triggering of the coil.

A third option is one of the systems that are fully integrated into a replacement distributor – a good option if your existing distributor is worn out.

Electronic ignition does provide a better-controlled spark, potentially a smoother advance curve, and should be 'fit and forget.' The downside is that if it fails, it tends to fail completely and can be difficult to repair – usually requiring the total replacement of components.

Unleaded cylinder head conversion

In the UK, leaded petrol has been phased out, and the exclusive use of unleaded fuel can cause valve seat recession on A-series engine cylinder heads. While it is still possible to buy separate fuel additives to address the situation, a permanent solution is to have the head modified to use hardened valve seats. Most good engineering shops can do

Under the bonnet of ADO16 lurks either a 1100 or 1300 A-series engine. Transversely mounted and with the gearbox in its sump, the packaging of the engine was unmatched.

Pretty much the last of the line in the UK was the 1300GT model. Here is John Norris' lovely Teal Blue example.

this, and if the car is being used a lot, it is probably worthwhile to have the seats replaced so the car will run happily on unleaded fuel.

Dynamo to alternator conversion

As standard, the 1100 was fitted with a positive earth electrical system with a dynamo and a mechanical control box to regulate the battery charge. While the system works well, it does not have much spare capacity, and as parts wear and connections corrode, the system can struggle to keep the battery fully charged when running with lights, wipers, and the heater fan going.

A simple solution is to replace the dynamo with an alternator. This is a simple bolt-on job that merely requires a new bracket to fix the alternator to the side of the engine and some minor wiring; essentially bypassing the control box as the alternator has a built-in voltage regulator. Using an alternator usually requires switching the cars to a negative earth system, a simple task.

Kit cars

While there were several Mini-based kit cars produced, the only

Probably the most popular kit car application for ADO16 was the Magenta. It was a new glassfibre bodyshell which used the front and rear subframes of ADO16 to produce a cross between a beach Buggy and a classic roadster.

In common with many contemporary kit cars, with the hood up, the Magenta had some weather protection, but looked somewhat ungainly.

significant one based on the 1100 and 1300 was the Lightspeed Panels Magenta. The Magenta hit the market in 1972 and was basically a new chassis and glassfibre bodyshell that took the ADO16 subframes and mechanical components, so it could be used to resurrect a rotted-out 1100 or 1300. The kit used the MG grille as well, giving a slightly bizarre-looking car – described as a 'Sports Tourer' by the maker. It was really a cross between a traditional roadster and a beach buggy!

Like all Mini-based kit cars, the Magenta's main issue was the height of the engine and gearbox unit, which tended to blunt the sporty lines with a high bonnet line. Otherwise, the kit was a creditable attempt to produce a fun, sporty car. Weather protection was minimal, and the lack of doors did limit the car's appeal to the enthusiast.

The Magenta capitalized on the mechanical strengths of ADO16 and provided a home for the mechanical elements of the many rusty ADO16s that abounded in the 1970s and 1980s, giving a relatively cheap and cheerful solution to the conundrum of scrap or save that so many owners of old and tatty examples of ADO16 faced.

The 1100 Club

As with most classic cars, the existence of a good, well-run club dedicated to the particular model is of major benefit for those owners who choose to run and restore the cars, and the ADO16 is no exception. The 1100 Club was formed in 1985 to serve the owners of ADO16s and was inspired by a very negative buyer's guide for ADO16 that featured in the popular UK magazine *Practical Classics*.

The 1100 Club's avowed goal was, and is, to keep the cars of existing members on the road and to provide new members with the advice and information to achieve the same aim. To this end, the club runs a nationwide network (the Hampshire area members helped with the production of this book, and four of its cars are featured) in the UK, which has local meetings, social functions, regular car meets, and technical support, as well as having a number of overseas members. The club also organizes an annual national rally, which includes concours competitions, car displays, and evening functions.

The club provides spares support to members, with a central spares coordinator, and makes great efforts to ensure that key spare parts are made available. Efforts to date include the production of new front wings and the tooling to produce lamp gaskets. The club also produces its own range of regalia, and members can also get discounts on a wide range of goods from insurance to motor oil.

Finally, the club produces a bi-monthly magazine, *Idle Chatter* – a full-colour, A4-sized publication full of articles on ADO16 – and also supports a very professional website, which includes a members-only area providing technical support, cars for sale, and every copy of *Idle Chatter* in downloadable format.

The 1100 Club is a popular, well-regarded and well-run club with lots of local and national events centred around ADO16. Here are John Norris' 1300 GT, Roy Robinson's Traveller, and David Haycock's Riley, with Dean Oakey's 1300 lurking in the background, all of which are featured in this book.

good (although Dean is only too happy to point out where it needs improvement), is a testament to his skills in keeping the car on the road.

It was not in such good shape when he bought it.

Owners' impressions

Dean Oakey's Morris 1300

Dean Oakey owns a 1971 Morris 1300 Mark II in Limeflower – a classic 1970 British Leyland pastel colour that suits the car. Dean is unusual as he uses his Morris as his daily driver, and when he bought it in 1998, he used it to develop his classic car mechanical skills. The fact that it is still running nicely and looks

Originally, he was looking for a Morris Minor to restore, and when he found an ad in the local paper for just such a car, he was around to the vendor like a shot.

However, while the car was a Morris, it was, in fact, a Morris 1300 – so the description was only 300cc out. The vendor was selling the car on behalf of his cousin who had moved to the USA – giving this story odd shades of the seller of David

Dean Oakey poses proudly with his daily driver Morris 1300.

Haycock's Riley (see Chapter 3). Is there something about ADO16s that sends a proportion of owners to the States?

However, despite the car not being a Minor, Dean was intrigued. He had some experience of the ADO16; his father owned one when Dean was a child, and he had fond memories of many happy family outings, which included an epic trip from Birmingham up to the wilds of Scotland, with Dean's Mum and Dad, and Dean's brother, with whom he shared the rear seat with a large Irish Setter.

The car did, in fact, sort of fill his brief, and the test drive showed it really did need restoration and would be the perfect car to learn restoration skills on: the brakes were seized, the doors were full of rust, as were the sills and wings, and the cherries on the cake were the seatbelts – they were fastened by tying a reef knot in the webbing. Oddly, despite all the very obvious faults, the car had just been given a new MOT test – which just shows that sometimes an MOT test is not worth the paper it's written on.

Dean was interested, though, and made a low offer, which

The rear three-quarter view of Dean's 1300 shows the no-nonsense styling of the Mark II model.

Dean Oakey's 1300 shows off its boot. Although it does not look that big, ADO16's boot was surprisingly spacious and helped to make the car a practical family conveyance.

the vendor, who was selling the car for his cousin in the USA, rebuffed, saying Dean would have to negotiate over the phone with the owner. Not being interested in trans-Atlantic negotiations, Dean walked away, but was surprised to be contacted a couple of days later, saying that his offer of half the asking price was acceptable, and so he went ahead and bought the car. And so his initiation into classic car ownership began!

Buying the car with the intention of learning maintenance and restoration skills meant that Dean was immediately on the bottom of a steep learning curve! Despite the car being his daily driver, welding was the first skill he needed to learn in order to

stop the car falling apart in front of his very eyes, so night school welding courses beckoned, and he quickly became competent in that black art – a necessary skill when restoring an ADO16.

Other skills were quickly learned from the inevitable Haynes manual, and Dean quickly learned the basics of keeping what is actually a relatively simple car running, while gradually improving it where needed.

Eventually, though, after seven years of rolling restoration, the car succumbed to the inevitable rust, and, in 2005, Dean took the car off the road for a major restoration. By then, the

Dean Oakey's Morris 1300 is a fine example of the breed. Still in use as a practical daily driver, Dean intends to continue using his example for as long as possible.

car needed major structural work, and Dean's welding skills were tested, with the fiddliest job being the replacement of the heel board onto which the rear subframe was mounted, while the biggest one was the extensive repairs needed to the front bulkhead.

The rotten doors were then repaired, and then the sills were replaced – a job that Dean had been dreading but which turned out to be relatively easy. New front wings and a front bumper mounting panel rounded off the welding, and then Dean had some luck when he was rear-ended, and the insurer agreed to fund the replacement of the rear panel. After all the work, the car needed a respray, and while he was initially not too keen on the original colour, Dean was persuaded to keep the car in Limeflower. He does not regret this, and now recognizes it was redolent of the car's 1970s history and is even beginning to quite like it.

The major restoration was completed within the year – Dean says thanks to his very understanding wife – and the car was back on the road for 2006 and has been there ever since.

Dean is not afraid to drive the car – in fact, it has been used as it was designed to be used: as a daily driver that can also do family holiday trips. And there have been some mega trips undertaken in the car, including the 2012 Lands End to John o'Groats to celebrate the 1100's 50th birthday, when the car was accompanied by many 1100 Club members from the UK, as well as an international contingent from France, Germany, and

Switzerland. While it was a grueling tour, putting in relatively long miles every day, all the cars completed it successfully.

Further tours included trips to France, in which Dean led the tour around the D-Day landing beaches, and has also toured the length of Ireland. On tour Dean gets around 40mpg, and the car's Hydrolastic suspension means it is comfortable and smooth even over long distances.

Even when using the car as a daily driver, Dean finds it easy to maintain, and any problems are easy to diagnose – there are no computers, laptops, and OBD ports needed here, just common sense and a modicum of mechanical knowledge.

Dean has had a few problems with the car (including blowing two head gaskets, which he attributes to being a bit too keen with the right foot), and has replaced one Hydrolastic unit, and a set of points ... which, for 20 odd years of motoring, is not bad at all. He also had the head modified to take unleaded fuel.

Dean's experience of restoring his car gave him some insights into the design. He believes that Mr Issigonis hadn't listened to the experts at BMC and managed to design in some rust traps that, with a little bit of thought, could have been avoided. He accepts that ADO16 does have a reputation for rusting but points out that most of the issues are, in fact, easily resolved, and modern-day rustproofing techniques work well and can mitigate most, if not all, of the major issues.

Dean sums up his 1300 as a labour of love. Having bought it as a basket case and learned all his classic car maintenance skills on its restoration, it's a part of him now, and of his family, especially with the memories of all the long-distance trips the family has made in it.

Having been resprayed some 17 years ago now, the car is showing its age a bit, although Dean is tougher on the car than he should be, as the car is in pretty good shape, despite a few rust bubbles and odds and sods that need doing. It is a car he would never consider selling, has never let him down, and Dean is planning another restoration this year, which will include the engine bay – even though it's looking pretty good – which will bring the car back up to an immaculate standard.

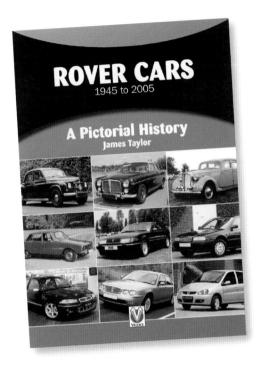

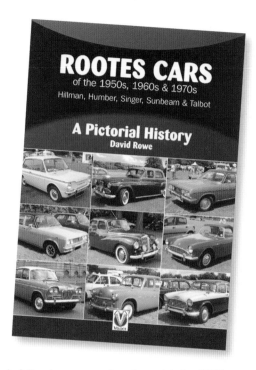

This comprehensive pictorial overview of Rover cars covers 1945-2005 models. It describes and illustrates all the great classic Rovers up to and including the SD1, British Leyland models with Rover badges, the models designed in conjunction with Honda, the later British-designed cars and, finally, the little-known City Rover.

The only full-colour comprehensive guide to all Hillman, Humber, Sunbeam, Singer & Talbot cars and vans, from 1950 until the end of production in the 1970s. With model-by-model descriptions and detailed technical information, this is an invaluable Rootes resource.

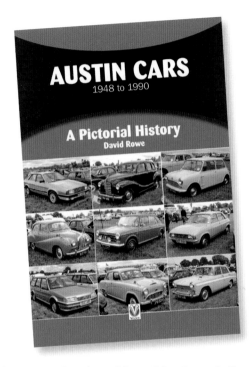

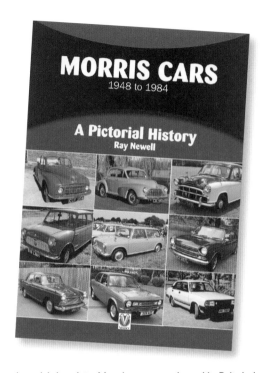

A full-colour comprehensive guide to all Austin cars built from 1948 until the end of production in the 1990s, with an informative history, detailed model-by-model comparisons, and technical information.

A handy guidebook to Morris cars produced in Britain between 1948 and 1984. Morris had been a prominent marque since it began production in 1913. Postwar Morris cars were exported around the world, and many were assembled in overseas plants. Although the last car was produced in 1984, many Morris models retain an enthusiastic following today.

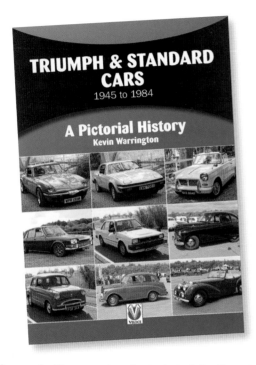

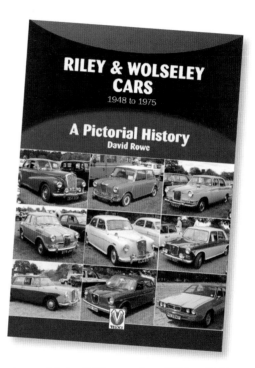

In full colour and with comprehensive technical detail, each model of car and light commercial produced and sold under the Standard and Triumph brands between 1945 and 1984 is illustrated and described in this new pictorial history. With crisp styling and solid mechanicals, these cars are fondly remembered by all enthusiasts.

A full colour guide to all Riley cars from 1953 to 1969 and Wolseley cars built from 1948 until 1975. With an informative history, detailed model-by-model comparisons and technical information, it is a comprehensive guide.

Index